Our Lady's Prophecies

Religious artist Dan O'Connell's painting of
The Miraculous Statue of Our Lady of Good Success of the Purification

Our Lady requested Mother Mariana to have Francisco del Castillo, a devout Catholic artist, sculpt a statue to be placed above the Abbess' chair. Annually the statue is carried in procession to the main altar for veneration by the public before and after the feast day of our Lady of Good Success of the Purification or Candlemas.

James M. Valois

Our Lady's Prophecies

God's Messages for Our Time

SOPHIA INSTITUTE PRESS
Manchester, New Hampshire

Sophia Institute Press
Box 5284, Manchester, NH 03108
1-800-888-9344
www.SophiaInstitute.com

Sophia Institute Press is a registered trademark of Sophia Institute.

paperback ISBN 979-8-88911-086-6

ebook ISBN 979-8-88911-087-3

Library of Congress Control Number: 2023947936

First printing

I dedicate this book with love to the Holy Family and to Don Paul, Maryann Christina, and Larry.

Acknowledgments

First of all, I would like to thank several family members for their encouragement and prayers during my work on this project. Furthermore, I would like to thank Heather Houle, Anna Maria Dube, and Patrick O'Hearn for their coordination of the project, excellent editing, collaborative spirit, and professionalism throughout the entire process. Finally, I am grateful to Sarah Lemieux and Mary Beth Bracy for their expertise and marketing savvy in the promotion of the book.

Contents

Foreword

WELL-INFORMED CATHOLICS TODAY AGREE that western culture is experiencing an unprecedented crisis of faith and morals. But many are only now discovering that the Blessed Virgin Mary prophesied the current situation in the Church and the world some four centuries ago. In a series of apparitions to a religious sister at the Royal Convent of the Immaculate Conception in Quito, Ecuador, Mary appeared as *La Nuestra Senora del Buen Suceso de la Purificación* (Our Lady of Good Success of the Purification) with a crucial message for our times.

When I first discovered Mary of Good Success around the turn of the century, there was little information available about her in English. Not that the devotion was secret or hidden, it was not. Rather, it was simply obscure. In fact, Our Lady told the visionary, Madre Mariana de Jesus Torres, that she would not become well-known under this title until the end of the 20th century. Not surprisingly, it was only in the 1980s that Mother Mariana's cause for beatification was finally opened and not until the 1990s that the book written by the postulator for her cause was translated into English.

In the book you are about to read, you will meet Servant of God Mariana of Jesus and learn of her remarkable encounters with Our Lady. The story includes miracles, human drama, inspiring examples of heroic virtue, and many prophecies. Some of the prophetic messages concern Ecuador, like the coming of a 19th century president who would be a model for modern Catholic politicians. But there are also many grave predictions concerning the dire situation in the Church and the world that have only been fulfilled in our own days. All is not "gloom and doom," however, for Mary also foretold that just when "all will seem lost and paralyzed" there will be a marvelous restoration of the Catholic Church.

But Jim Valois does more than vividly recount the story of this devotion. In addition, he connects the prophecies and promises entrusted to Mother Mariana with subsequent historical events — and the details of other approved Marian apparitions — to powerfully demonstrate the urgent significance of her message for Catholics today.

Since my first pilgrimage to Quito in 2007, I have promoted devotion to Our Lady of Good Success at parishes, retreats, and Marian conferences on four continents. At each one of those events, I have related the promise of the Blessed Virgin to grant her "good success" to all who would promote this devotion, in her words, "In the time to come when I desire to be known."

As Jim Valois compellingly reveals, that time is now.

Matthew Arnold
Garden Grove, 2023

Our Lady's Prophecies

Introduction

You ARE ABOUT TO read many startling prophecies concerning the current crisis in the Church and the world. Our Lady of Good Success of the Purification gave these messages over four hundred years ago, roughly one hundred years after Christopher Columbus sailed for the New World and discovered America. They happened around 1582 in Quito, the capital city of Ecuador, when it was the colony of St. Francisco of Quito. Shortly after Our Lady appeared, Bishop Salvador Ribera Avalos approved the messages in 1611, which have been upheld by every Ecuadorian bishop since that time.

Our Lady's messages to Mother Mariana de Jesus Torres are eye-opening, hard-hitting, and enlightening. Even though this apparition took place many years ago, these messages are now more important than ever because they touch on the coming restoration. Specifically, several prophecies foretold twentieth-century and twenty-first-century events. These events happened during the period when the invention of clock-making was still flourishing throughout Europe and Spain was still sending vessels across the ocean to the New World.

Similar to Our Lady of Fatima's prophecies, Our Lady of Good Success of the Purification's messages of hope shine through the darkness of our troubled times. These revelatory messages reveal and predict the blatant attacks on the Church, the sacraments, the priesthood, and the family. They highlight the radical changes in customs and the shocking state of our modern world as seen through the eyes of a humble, holy nun — Servant of God Mariana de Jesus Torres. In fact, the shock was so great that Mother Mariana died when she saw it! But thanks be to God, she was raised back to life and offered her life as a victim soul to protect her sisters during the crisis in the twentieth century and beyond.

Rather than cover every prophecy given by Our Lady of Good Success, this book will focus on those that concern our times and those that have already come to fulfillment. The latter helps authenticate these prophecies, thus increasing our belief in their relevance for today. The term *prophecy* can mean several things, especially as seen in Scripture. A prophet often accurately described the spiritual condition of the people and sometimes foretold future events. In this book, prophecy refers to those messages given to Mother Mariana by Our Lady concerning future events.

When I visited Quito, Ecuador as an evangelical, I learned about a former president, a man of great faith from the country's modern period. At the time of my visit, I was unaware that this truly devout Catholic president was the fulfillment of a specific prophecy given to Mother Mariana 261 years before his first term as president of Ecuador in 1860.

I ask that you read these prophetic messages with an open mind. After all, we are called to hear the proclamation of the kingdom and then respond with ongoing conversion. Time is short and the stakes are very high. Hence Christ calls us to daily conversion, as the third Luminous Mystery of the Rosary reminds us. These messages call us to conversion too. They exhort us to prayer and sacrifice, just like at Fatima.

May you be renewed, enlightened, and encouraged by our loving Mother's messages. Our Mother — whom Jesus gave to the Church to intercede for us — will help us through the challenges and tribulations on this side of the veil.

CHAPTER ONE

The Perilous Journey

A Vision at Sea

A LIGHT RAIN FELL on the small wooden ship that left Spain bound for the New World and the colony of Ecuador. The journey would take about two months, depending on weather conditions. The year was 1576. Philip II, king of Spain, authorized six passengers on board for a spiritual mission. These passengers on the Spanish vessel, about the size of a mid-size yacht by today's standards, were Mother Maria de Jesus Taboada, her young niece (Mariana Francisca Torres y Berriochoa), and four other nuns. Their love for God inspired them to build a convent in San Francisco de Quito, a city set over the ruins of an Incan metropolis.

Almost twenty years previous, the devout matrons of Quito requested that the civil and ecclesiastical officials allow the Spanish Order of Nuns of the Immaculate Conception of Blessed Mary to establish a convent in the city.[1] These devout women of faith, along with the first bishop and town council, sent the request to King Phillip II of Spain since the religious order was under his patronage.[2]

In his book, *The Story of Our Lady of Good Success and Novena,* Fr. Manuel Sousa Pereira indicates that Quito's leaders also saw value in creating a convent for nuns: "The authorities saw the benefit of founding a convent where they would gather together poor girls, *mestizos* and Spanish daughters of the Conquistadors for their spiritual life."[3] Writer Hon. Mrs. Maxwell-Scott explains the unity that existed among the first Spanish settlers and Ecuadorians in the colony: "At first the Spanish kings did their duty faithfully to their new possessions. Bishops and priests were sent to evangelize the country, and civilization and religion united to secure its prosperity, but in the following century everything was changed."[4]

En route to the colony, suddenly the rain started to pour, and a terrifying storm broke out as the small Spanish vessel was deep out at sea. Lightning and thunder repeated their cycles like cannon fire in the tempest. The ship was taking on water as it was tossed about and was in danger of sinking. Even the sailors were afraid that the voyage was doomed.

The nuns prayed fervently on deck. Amid the tumult, Mother Maria and her niece, Mariana, had a startling vision of a gigantic sea serpent in the ocean that was attempting to destroy the vessel. The thirteen-year-old Mariana fainted. When Mariana regained consciousness, she and Mother Maria heard a horrible voice shout at them over the noise of the seas: "I will not permit this foundation. I will not permit it to go forward. I will not permit it to endure until the end of time, and I will persecute it unceasingly."[5] The evil one was obviously threatening to wage war against the holy nuns.

Following this vision, Mother Maria and Mariana witnessed another, more breathtaking event. Dr. Marian Horvat writes:

> As the waves threatened to swallow the ship, they witnessed the [appearance] of the Holy Virgin who carried the Child Jesus in her right arm. He carried a sword that he used to slash the heads of the serpent to pieces. To keep this event ever present in the memory of future generations of nuns, Mother Maria ordered a round scapular with this formidable vision of the Virgin and Child defeating the serpent to be made. The Conceptionists of the Royal Monastery in Quito continue to this day to wear the insignia on their habits as a lasting reminder of the momentous event.[6]

The sea became tranquil immediately after Jesus and Mary appeared. Mother Maria and Mariana knew who was behind the tempest and why the storm abruptly ended. Just as Jesus once calmed the stormy Sea of Galilee for His apostles (see Matt. 8:23–27), He intervened once again.

The Early Life of Mariana Francisca Torres y Berriochoa

Mariana Francisca's mystical experiences at sea were not a first. Her early life was also noteworthy and filled with supernatural revelations. Mariana was the oldest child of pious and noble parents, Diego Torres Cadiz and Maria Berriochoa Alvaro. Mariana had two younger brothers. The family lived in a small village in the Basque province of Vizcaya. Located in a rural setting, farm fields and grape groves provided the main sources of income. Since the family home was next to the parish church, little Mariana would run in to be with Jesus in the tabernacle during part of her playtime.[7]

Mariana had a sweet disposition. Specifically, God had "endowed her with beauty, a quick intelligence, a sweet nature and a strong inclination toward virtue."[8] She also had a strong love for our eucharistic Lord and would sing new songs to Jesus that she learned from Scripture. "There an unsuspected happiness flooded little Mariana's soul as she offered Jesus the canticles that she learned."[9]

When Mariana was seven years old, another harrowing event occurred. Her parish priest entrusted the church to the sacristan when he traveled on family business. The sacristan decided to take advantage of the good weather and do some farm work. Prior to working outside, he filled the sanctuary lamp to the brim with oil. Tragically, an earth tremor caused it to overturn, and a huge fire broke out in the church while the sacristan was in the fields. The fire spread rapidly, obliterating the church, Mariana's home, outbuildings, and other property. Fortunately, the family survived, but the fire was devastating to the family's finances. They moved to Santiago in

Galicia, and the saintly Mariana could no longer visit Jesus in the tabernacle because the new church was too far away.[10]

In Santiago, a Franciscan friar gave special permission for nine-year-old Mariana to receive her First Holy Communion. The usual age for the sacrament was thirteen or fourteen at that time. Receiving Jesus for the first time was an occasion of great joy for the young mystic. During an ecstasy, the Blessed Mother revealed to Mariana that she was destined to be a religious of the Immaculate Conception. Later, she learned that her aunt, Mother Maria de Jesus Taboada, was leaving Spain for a foundation in the Americas. Mariana heard Jesus speak to her at Communion: "Leave behind your country and the house of your parents, because the King of Heaven is enamored with your beauty."[11] Mariana's parents did not object to her entering the Conceptionists as long as she stayed in Spain. But Mariana loved the Lord first, and she wanted to follow His call to the missionary colony. Four years later, Mariana embarked for Ecuador with her aunt and the other nuns.

Another Perilous Trek

The city of San Francisco de Quito is an interesting place. Residents say that you can experience all four seasons in one day: spring in the morning, summer in the afternoon, fall in the late afternoon and early evening, and winter at night. Located 9,350 feet above sea level and set in a valley between the eastern and western range of the Andes Mountains, Quito's unique spot causes these temperature variations. The air is thinner, but the altitude does not affect every person adversely. The people of the region seem warm and friendly.

When Mother Maria, Mariana, and the other nuns landed on the coast, they faced another difficult trek inland to their destination. There was no infrastructure at the time. It took several centuries before a great Catholic president would build roadways. Writer Peter Henderson explains that even two hundred years later — in the 1830s — the journey from the coastal city of Guayaquil to Quito was a rough one:

Riding on a horse from Guayaquil to Quito was not exactly a pleasant experience in the 1830s. Although horse and mule trains regularly plied the [so-called] "Royal Road" once every two weeks (less frequently during the rainy season), the 320-mile, 21-day journey entailed considerable hardships.[12]

Other travelers testify to the challenging travel conditions in Ecuador before the 1870s:

> An English tourist, when asked by what road he had managed to reach Quito, replied, "But there is no question of roads in this country" and an adventurous lady traveler remarks [sic] in her book that "on leaving the Capital of Ecuador, one does not drive, one only paddles through a morass."[13]

When the Spanish foundress and her five companions reached the coast of Ecuador, they had to walk the long and arduous way to the inland city. According to Msgr. Cadena y Almeida, it was no easy task:

> To reach Quito, the nuns valiantly scaled a rough and arid mountain range over 9,000 feet high through brush, over creeks, up depthless precipices. During this exhausting trek, they encountered countless hardships and dark sleepless nights spent in fear amid the howling of wild animals.[14]

Because these religious loved the Lord, they endured these trials with a spirit of self-sacrifice and devotion to the King of Heaven, who protected them.

Finally, the foundresses reached San Francisco de Quito. Msgr. Cadena y Almeida describes the beautiful scene:

> At last, on the morning of December 30, 1576, the nuns, with worn-out feet and aching bodies, trudged into Quito.

> The joy of the people and the sound of trumpets and drums that resounded throughout the countryside proclaimed the triumph of the frail maidens. With full and joyous hearts ready to scale the mountains of love, the Conceptionist sisters sang a *Te Deum* in thanksgiving for this second battle won for God.[15]

After being welcomed by the civil and religious authorities, the Conceptionist sisters were taken to their convent — the first convent of cloistered nuns in the colony.

St. Beatriz de Silva of Portugal founded the Order of the Immaculate Conception, a branch of the Franciscan Order of St. Clare, in 1482. The Virgin Mary appeared to Beatriz and asked her to found the order: *"Beatriz, I would like you to found a new Order in honor of my Immaculate Conception, [whose religious will be] clothed with a white habit and blue mantle as I wear."*[16] That is why the Quito convent was initially under the Franciscans and why these sisters wear a white habit with a sky-blue mantle.

As the convent was being established, local Indian women soon joined the Conceptionsits' cloister. Within these hallowed walls, young Mariana's vocation would blossom. Here she would receive some of the most stunning revelations.

CHAPTER TWO

Vision of the Three Swords

Sr. Mariana: A Victim Soul

THE ANTICIPATED DAY FOR Mariana's entrance into the Conceptionists' novitiate (this is a beginning phase of entrance into religious life) had finally arrived. The fourteen-year-old Mariana now donned her order's white and blue habit, further distancing herself from the world. Franciscan Friar Antonio Jurado celebrated the special Mass. At the Offertory, "her aunt, the Mother Abbess, symbolically divested her of all the youthful feminine attire that accented the freshness and innocence of her youthful face."[17] The new novice would follow the same schedule for prayer, penances, work, and reflection as the professed nuns for two years. After this trial period ended, the community voted on whether a sister should proceed for vows.

During her novitiate, Mariana studied and lived out the rule of the Conceptionist Order. After the period of discernment for both Mariana and her community, Msgr. Cadena y Almeida explained the next step in the process:

> After two years, the time came for her to take the simple vows, which allow the novice the option of repeating them at a later date or not, depending on whether she, after serious reflection, feels the necessary moral strength to continue fulfilling them for life.[18]

Instead of taking simple vows, Mariana, her superiors, and her community felt she was ready for final vows. After final vows, Mariana would remain in the cloister for the remainder of her earthly life. Her chosen name was Sr. Mariana de Jesus. The date set for her final vows was October 4, 1579, the feast of St. Francis of Assisi, who was called to go and rebuild the Church in the thirteenth century.

The liturgy for final vows was well-planned. First, there was plenty of light from the candles and oil lamps. These appropriate symbols and expressions are utilized to introduce the candidate to the heavenly reality without negating the world's misery surrounding the convent walls.[19] When the time came for Sr. Mariana de Jesus to make her profession, she experienced an ecstasy. Fr. Pereira describes the experience:

> She saw Jesus, whom she was espousing, placing on her right hand a ring of precious stones. Jesus said to her, among other things, "Your life will be a continual martyrdom." [Sr.] Mariana de Jesus accepted, pleased and grateful, and Jesus promised to help her.[20]

Jesus chose Sr. Mariana as a victim soul. In the twentieth century, Jesus chose other victim souls like St. Padre Pio. He bore the stigmata for fifty years and encountered all sorts of attacks and sufferings as a victim soul for the benefit of numerous souls. Sr. Mariana was also invited to be a victim soul not only for her times but also for the Church crisis that would emerge in the 1960s and 1970s.

At the same time Jesus asked Sister Mariana to be a victim soul, He also prophesized to her and lovingly accepted her as His spouse. He showed her the convent through the centuries, trials in her life, and a significant crisis that would happen in the convent. Jesus also told her that a certain holy nun in the future would suffer from leprosy and have to move to a leper colony. There she would be a shining example of charity and joy. This future sister — another victim soul — would protect the convent and country from greater chastisements due to the many secret and public crimes in that century.[21]

Sr. Mariana embraced her special mission of penance, guided by Jesus Himself. "When her aunt and prioress, Mother Maria de Jesus, asked her to mention to Our Lord her concern for her [niece's] health, Jesus answered Mother Mariana that after her penances she would be fresh and vigorous, and so it was," Fr. Pereira explained.[22] Many will recall from Sacred Scripture how the prophet Daniel and his companions, appointed to government positions in Babylon, would not eat the pagan meats in fidelity to the Law. Daniel had asked the steward to run a test of who would be healthier after he and his companions ate vegetables and the other men ate the king's rich food. Scripture tells us: "At the end of ten days it was seen that they [men of Israel] were better in appearance and fatter in flesh than all the youths who eat the king's rich food" (Dan. 1:15–16). As promised by Our Lord, Sr. Mariana became renewed and even healthier after her penances.

In our era of comfort-seeking and instant gratification, we often fail to see the redemptive value of penance. Sister Mariana had a special calling and guidance from Jesus in her penances. While prayer and sacrifice should be part of every Christian's life, some are invited to go above and beyond for the sake of others. Dr. Marian Horvat rightly points out concerning Sr. Mariana's penances: "Her severe disciplines, sacrifices, fasting and prayer, all described in the chapters of the manuscript, appear daunting to the man of our century, who finds suffering something to avoid or, at best, to endure as grudgingly as possible."[23]

As Sister Mariana continued her formation, she was assigned many different roles over the years. As a nurse, she took care of the sisters who were sick or injured. Once a sister received a life-threatening burn on the face and arm, and when Sr. Mariana prayed for her, God cured the sister. The doctor was amazed.

Another assigned role was purveyor. Here, Sister was tasked with the needs of the convent. When food was short, Sr. Mariana would go to Jesus in the tabernacle and bread would multiply or alms would arrive. Other duties included sacristan, liaison to those outside the cloister, assistant to the choir master, and mistress of novices.[24] In all these roles, Sr. Mariana applied herself with great love, dedication, and virtue. Since Sr. Mariana was elected abbess of the convent on several occasions, we shall henceforth use the term Mother Mariana for the sake of simplicity.

Mother Mariana before the Tabernacle in 1582

One night in 1582, Mother Mariana was praying before the tabernacle. Light emanated from the tabernacle; it opened, and Jesus Crucified came out from it. The Virgin, St. John, and St. Mary Magdalene, all life-size, were at His feet. When Jesus began to be in agony, the little nun asked the Virgin if she was guilty, and the Virgin replied, "You are not guilty, but rather the sinful world." Then the voice of God the Eternal Father was heard: "This punishment will be for the twentieth century." Next, three swords appeared above Jesus' head. On each sword was written the following words: heresy, blasphemy, and impurity. Mother Mariana also received knowledge of twentieth-century events and beyond. The Virgin asked her if she would sacrifice herself for the people of the twentieth century. Mother willingly accepted. Then the swords in the vision plunged into her heart and she fell dead.[25]

Dr. Sancho, the doctor for the nuns, was called, and he declared Mother Mariana dead. Similar to a near-death experience, where a person dies and enters eternal realms and then returns to his body, Mother Mariana came back to life. The Father Superior asked her to explain everything that happened. Mother Mariana provided Father with specific details:

> Mother Mariana had indeed died and now stood before
> the judgment seat of God, Who found no fault in her and
> invited her to receive the crown prepared for her since the

beginning of the world. At the same time, her distraught sisters implored Heaven to restore the life of this exemplary religious.[26]

Mother received a revelation about the Holy Trinity and God's deep love for her:

> She was presented to the Holy Trinity, and she understood part of that mystery. The Father rejoiced for having created her, the Son for having redeemed her and the Holy Ghost for having sanctified her.[27]

Revelation was also given by Our Lady regarding the future sisters of the convent, the faithful and unfaithful, and her future role as mistress of novices. Other prophetic knowledge and consolations were imparted to Mother Mariana.[28]

Then she was offered two crowns. One was the crown of life to remain in Heaven, and the other was a crown of lilies surrounded with thorns. Mother faced a decision: to remain in Heaven or return to earth. Although she wanted to stay in Heaven, Our Lady invited her to follow her example, and Mother Mariana chose to return to earth to help her sisters.[29] Mother agreed to be a victim soul for our times. But how might we understand her vision of the three swords and its written message for our age?

Heresy

The punishments or chastisements focus on three major rebellions that persist today, the first being heresy. A Catholic encyclopedia offers this helpful definition of heresy:

> Heretic comes from a Greek word that means "picking and choosing." We can legitimately pick and choose in many contexts, but not in regard to what God has revealed. To do so would mean setting up one's own judgment as the final

standard and gauge of truth in matters of salvation, and re-
fusing to accept that Jesus Christ established His Church as
possessor and teacher of His truth.[30]

In essence, heresy defines salvific truths according to our own ideas
versus divine revelation.

A major heresy or false teaching in our epoch is communism.
This worldview always promises Heaven on earth in a utopian fan-
tasy, but instead, it has delivered unparalleled violence and bloodshed. Some experts believe that communism killed the most people
in the twentieth century, as conveyed by writer John Walters:

> Communism was the leading ideological cause of death
> between 1900 and 2000. The 94 million that perished in
> China, the Soviet Union, North Korea, Afghanistan, and
> Eastern Europe easily (and tragically) trump the 28 million
> that died under fascist regimes during the same period.[31]

Other experts place the total number of deaths higher. Unfortunately,
it underscores the valid point that false teaching has real-world
consequences.

The popes have consistently warned of the evils of communism.
For example, Cardinal Pacelli, before he was Pope Pius XII, visited the
United States in 1936 and warned FDR of "a 'great danger' of communism in America, which FDR naively dismissed."[32] Pius XI, in his 1931
encyclical *Quadragesimo Anno,* wrote: "Socialism (is) irreconcilable
with true Christianity. Religious socialism, Christian socialism, are
contradictory terms; no one can be at the same time a good Catholic
and a true socialist."[33] Also in *Divini Redemptoris,* an intense examina-
tion of the atheistic system, Pius XI called communism "a 'collectivistic
terrorism' threatening the world, a 'savage barbarity', a pernicious
'plague' promulgated by Marxist 'powers of darkness.' Mincing no
words, the Catholic Church called communism a 'satanic scourge.'"[34]

This is only a small sampling of what the popes have taught about this quasi-futuristic system of so-called "equality."

According to Fr. Andrew Apostoli, CFR, Our Lady of Fatima's apparition on July 13, 1917 centered on the errors of communism:

> In that very important apparition of July 13, our Lady warned the children about the evils of communism, which would begin in Russia and spread its errors throughout the world. She also said that communism would cause wars and persecutions of the Church.[35]

The revelations given to both Mother Mariana and the Fatima children predicted key errors of our times. Pope St. John Paul II connected these errors with the brutal attacks on humanity. Again, Fr. Apostoli wrote:

> Pope John Paul II fittingly said that at Fatima our Lady foretold the main events of the twentieth century, a century characterized by extreme violence and the greatest destruction of human life that the world has ever seen. The threat of communism and its many offspring remains to this day.[36]

Regarding the threat of communism today, we need look no further than the Chinese Communist Party (CCP). The CCP's aggressive actions have led to the persecution of its own people, particularly many religious groups. The United States Commission on International Religious Freedom reports:

> Religious freedom conditions in China continue to deteriorate. The communist Chinese government has created a high-tech surveillance state, utilizing facial recognition and artificial intelligence to monitor and harass Christians, Tibetan Buddhists, Falon Gong and other religions. Independent experts estimate that between 900,000 and 1.8 million Uyghur, Kazakh, Kyrgyz, and other Muslims

have been detained in more than 1,300 concentration camps in Xinjiang.[37]

Despite the CCP's sinister crimes against humanity, several western corporations and even governments partner with them, thus ignoring such egregious crimes. It is well past time to face the truth and avoid doing business with the CCP until they stop these crimes. Unfortunately, many western countries are embracing socialism and communism.

Russia's errors have clearly spread globally, producing the same bad fruits everywhere: abortion-on-demand, the rejection of religion in public discourse, the destruction of the family, and the secularization of all moral issues. The second message on the sword identifies another serious offense in our days — blasphemy.

Blasphemy

In 2014, Adam Daniels, an Oklahoma Satanist, claimed to have consecrated Hosts in his possession. He planned to hold a black mass at the Oklahoma City Civic Center. When this became public, Archbishop Paul Coakley of the Diocese of Oklahoma City urged civic officials to cancel the contract for the facility. After this attempt failed, Archbishop Coakley then took Daniels to court over stolen Church property — namely, the consecrated Hosts. The Satanic ritual desecrates and blasphemes the Hosts in the black mass. The archdiocesan lawsuit stated:

> The specific Satanic ritual known as a "black mass" is intended as a deliberate attack on the Catholic Mass as well as the foundational beliefs of all Christians with the stated purpose of mocking the Catholic faith. As well, the statement of claim argued the consecrated Hosts were the property of the Catholic Church obtained by theft or false pretense.[38]

Fortunately, Daniels agreed to return the consecrated Hosts and the archdiocese agreed to drop the suit. But it does show that blasphemy and desecration attempts are becoming even more public now.

In a conversation with Fr. Timothy Welles, a Midwest pastor, he credited the rise of blasphemy today to the increase in various addictions. He explained that sins are often found in clusters. One example would be a person suffering from alcoholism who curses God when he drinks. This connection between addictions and blasphemy seems clear as one of the reasons for the increase of the latter. So, what is blasphemy?

Fr. Apostoli explained blasphemy and the priority of turning from it as the first thing we must do:

> What are the sins we must turn away from? First, the sins of blasphemy, which are directed against God, our Lady, the angels and saints and those things that are sacred because they are associated with the honor and worship of God. Such offenses express an actual, even if indirect, hatred of God. These sins must be overcome by the lively faith of believers, along with their authentic love of God and neighbor.... Remember, God's love is stronger than the world's hatred.[39]

The Catechism of the Catholic Church (CCC) further defines blasphemy in this way:

> It consists in uttering against God — inwardly or outwardly — words of hatred, reproach, or defiance; in speaking ill of God; in failing in respect toward him in one's speech; in misusing God's name. St. James condemns those "who blaspheme that honorable name [of Jesus] by which you are called." (CCC 2148)

Prior to his conversion, St. Paul was a perfect example of a blasphemer when he persecuted Jesus by persecuting His Church (see 1 Tim. 1:13).

The CCC also reveals some important but lesser-known aspects of blasphemy:

> It is also blasphemous to make use of God's name to cover up criminal practices, to reduce peoples to servitude, to torture persons or put them to death. The misuse of God's name to commit a crime can provoke others to repudiate religion. (CCC 2148)

The filth of impurity is another terrible sin that causes much destruction in our world. Let us examine it more closely.

Impurity

One of the leading causes of impurity today is pornography. Consider the proliferation of porn in our technological age. The Road to Purity website (roadtopurity.com) traces the recent roots of the epidemic:

> Porn began to explode with the introduction of *Playboy* magazine in 1953. This was a major contributing factor to the sexual revolution in the 1960's. Follow that with the introduction of high-speed internet in the early 2000's and in 2007, the iPhone was introduced. That same year, *Pornhub*, the world's second largest porn developer, was launched.[40]

Rationalizations, excuses, and failed leadership have led to the current widespread plague of impurity.

The scope of the crisis is massive, and the number of people suffering from it is staggering. Think about these data points:

✣ Porn teaches that "sex is not a gift; it's something to be taken" (revealed in the fact that 88 percent of porn demonstrates physical aggression).

✠ *Pornhub* reports an average of 120–150 million visitors daily worldwide.

✠ Total porn user base is estimated at 300–400 million visitors daily.

✠ A report by the Kaiser Family Research Foundation shows that there is an average of 143 incidents of sexual behavior on prime-time network TV each week (not cable, not pay per view, but on network TV). And 97 percent of these sexual situations were between non-married individuals.

✠ Sixty-seven percent of men aged 18–35 engage in porn weekly.

✠ Eleven million teens view porn daily.

✠ The average age of first exposure is nine years old.[41]

Although these statistics paint a hopeless picture, this is another illusion of the devil. All is not lost. God is raising up a bulwark of Christian organizations to combat pornography and help individuals addicted to it.

Another shocking fact is the growing acceptance of pornography among young women. The violent nature of porn makes this reality even more troubling. Consider these stats:

✠ According to a study published in the *Journal of Adolescent Research, about half (49 percent)* of young adult women agree that viewing pornography is an *acceptable* way of expressing one's sexuality.

✠ About *1 in 5 women (18 percent)* use the Internet for sexual purposes habitually — *every week.*[42]

Pornography is a serious problem for both men and women. Let us review some of the reasons why it is wrong.

"Simply put, pornography destroys human dignity and God's gift of sexuality. Every person has value and is worthy of great respect, and is entitled to be free from slavery, manipulation or exploitation," says the ministry Road to Purity.[43] Clearly, pornography opposes the virtue of chastity, the family, and the commandments because sin harms us and others (see CCC 2211, 2354, 2396).

Substantial evidence exists showing that "human trafficking and sex slavery is heavily linked to pornography" and "porn use is progressive and a dress rehearsal for prostitution."[44] Rape and child porn are also a big issue in the porn industry. "The biggest online distributor (currently) of porn has 17 lawsuits against it for rape, child porn and more," stated Steve Pokorny of Freedom Coaching.[45]

The Catholic understanding of freedom involves doing what is right and just, not whatever we please, which is false freedom. Christian freedom brings peace; the false notion of freedom leads to bondage. Scripture manifests this truth, and human experience confirms it: "For freedom Christ has set us free; stand fast therefore, and do not submit again to a yoke of slavery" (Gal. 5:1). In Christian freedom, we choose the good while sin enslaves us, bringing misery upon ourselves and others.

Many souls today are ensnared by impurity and servitude, but it does not need to stay that way. God wants us to possess "the glorious liberty of the children of God" (Rom. 8:21), which flows from doing what is just.

The prior reflections concerning the three swords messages are not exhaustive; many heresies, blasphemies, and forms of impurity infect our age. We must pray and cling to our Catholic Faith to avoid the rebellions of heresy, blasphemy, and impurity. Let us now look at the account of the miraculous statue and other revelations given.

CHAPTER THREE

The Miraculous Statue

The First Apparition of Our Lady
of Good Success of the Purification

AFTER THE DEATH OF the first abbess, Mother Maria de Jesus Taboada, in 1593, Mother Mariana was elected abbess at age thirty. Saddened by the loss of her aunt and spiritual formator, God told her that Mother Maria went to Heaven shortly after her death.[46] When Mother Mariana was installed as the second abbess, a stranger came and delivered a treat for the nuns to celebrate her election and said:

> "The lady, knowing that Mother Mariana de Jesus was elected prioress, sent her this treat, asking that she always be mindful of her." The gift was so large that it took several nuns to carry it. Mother Mariana smiled ... and shared among the religious the treat, which was exquisite and seemed to never run out. The next day ... Maria of Solanda, benefactress of the convent, sent presents and went in person ... to congratulate Mother Mariana. Mother Mariana thanked her for the treat of the previous day ... but the marchioness assured her that she was not the one who had sent it; then Mother Mariana understood that it was the Virgin herself who had sent the gift.[47]

At the time Mariana was chosen to be the abbess, trouble began brewing in Quito. During the colony's infancy, many dedicated Spaniards settled there and sought to educate and provide religious formation for the indigenous people. These Christians understood the mission to evangelize and better the lives of the native people. But things changed quickly when corrupt men seeking gold and control later moved to the colony. Dr. Horvat describes the situation at that period: "Adventurers ... are crazed by the desire for gold and power. These men created a pretext for revolt among the native people of Quito against the Crown of Spain."[48]

Yet it would be a distortion of history to discount the many good Spaniards who served the natives heroically in line with the good Catholic kings' and the original missionaries' intentions.

Mother faced many trials at the time, including monetary and obedience problems. Specifically, the community faced a serious issue surrounding the observance of the rule by a group of native sisters led by a nun called *the Captain*. Because of the manipulations by the *Captain*, the nuns experienced the threat of separation from the Franciscans' spiritual direction.[49] To make matters worse, Spain was sending over a mixed bag of religious — some seeking a more lax monastic life and some who wanted to live entirely for God and others.[50] Yet Mother Mariana knew her Savior could be completely trusted, so as usual, she took these concerns to Jesus in the tabernacle to seek His wisdom. It was February 2, 1594, when the event took place.

Bowing her forehead to the ground in the upper choir, Mother implored God's intervention for her convent's many problems. She then heard a sweet voice call her name and saw a beautiful lady wearing the Conceptionists' habit with its white tunic and blue mantle.

In her left arm was a beautiful child. In her right hand, she carried a scepter of gold set with precious stones.[51] Mother Mariana told her confessor later that "her soul was flooded with a holy and ineffable joy and an intense love for her Lord and God."[52] Mother Mariana asked the Lady who she was and what she wished. The Lady responded:

I am Mary of Good Success, Queen of heaven and earth. It is precisely because you are a religious soul who loves God and your Mother that I now speak to you. I have come from heaven to console your afflicted heart. Your prayers, tears and penances are very pleasing to our heavenly Father who imbues you with His consoling Spirit. God the Father, Who is the support of the just in their tribulations, has formed from three drops of blood from my heart the most beautiful child of man.[53]

Our Lady was referring to her Son as the most beautiful Child of man, as the message clarifies. Mary also explained her mediating role in seeking mercy for sinners. Mary also explained her mediating role in divine justice given to rebellious men. Furthermore, Our Lady explained that the scepter symbolizes the Virgin's wish to govern the Quito convent as abbess and mother. This message thus fulfilled the prophecy that the Friars Minor would soon withdraw from guiding the convent. Furthermore, these diabolical attacks (the Franciscans leaving and divisions in the convent) would not last forever because of Our Lady's intervention.[54]

Our Lady also promised that the Conceptionists would be victorious over all her enemies — present and future. The Conceptionists of Quito faced evictions, revolutions, and many other attacks through the centuries, but they have always been protected. In fact, Madre Ines, the abbess of the Conceptionist convent in Quito from our era, related a recent account of divine protection to Catholic apologist and author Matthew Arnold:

Madre Ines told me how, in a recent situation, the government regime had ordered the sisters to leave the convent. The Jesuits appealed to the courts to try and stop the action, but to no avail. On the appointed day, the sisters prayed the Little Office of the Blessed Virgin Mary (as Mother Mariana and her nuns also did) and waited for the soldiers to come and evict them. And they waited … and they waited. But the soldiers never came. Because that day, the regime fell. Our Lady promised that this convent would survive until the end of the world.[55]

Returning to the first apparition, Our Lady, the heavenly abbess of the convent, encouraged Mother Mariana with her maternal intercession. Specifically, the Virgin said the continued apparitions would be "like strong and stout columns, they will sustain the community in troubled times. [The Conceptionists'] life of prayer, self-denial and penance will be most needed during each period."[56] Before the end of the apparition, Our Lady allowed Mother Mariana to hold the baby Jesus in her arms, and this gave Mother such great joy.

Chosen a Second Time

Although Mother Mariana was looking forward to stepping down from leading the convent after her three-year term as abbess expired in 1597, the sisters chose her again as abbess for a second term. The disunity and distrust in the colony at the time was a result of the power-hungry adventurers seeking fortunes at the expense of the people. This spilled over into the convent when the small nun they called *the Captain* wanted the convent to relax the rule. The machination began with *the Captain* working with her priest-relative in the chancery office to separate the Franciscan Friars from the convent. This all happened when the bishop was traveling in his large diocese. Then she began sowing discord among the native sisters who did not have much of an education and were easily led.[57] In time, *the Captain* succeeded in having Mother Mariana removed from her office as abbess and even imprisoned by bringing false charges. But Mother accepted the trial with tears, patience, and serenity.

The other foundresses could see through these false charges because they knew Mother Mariana was innocent. However, since the zealous Bishop Luis Lopez de Solis was frequently traveling, the vicar general was in charge, and he believed the accusations of *the Captain* against her superior. The plan to relax the rule began to unfold.[58]

Our Lady then appeared to Mother Mariana to strengthen and console her amid these trials. Our Lady promised her patronage and protection would be even more crucial given the Franciscans' imminent departure. Our Lady of Good Success of the Purification spoke to Mother:

> "With this (removal of the Franciscans)," she said, "Satan will begin to try to destroy this work of God, making use of my ungrateful daughters, but he will not succeed, because I am the Queen of Victories and the Mother of Good Success, and under this invocation I desire to be known throughout time for the preservation of my Convent and its inhabitants."[59]

Eventually, the truth came out and the bishop restored her as abbess. In future years, Mother fondly remembered these trying times because of Our Lady's unfailing protection in stifling Satan's plans.

Mother Mariana, the other foundresses, and several sisters maintained courage amid the numerous diabolical attacks on the convent, false charges made against them to Church officials, and other injustices leveled directly at their faith. These holy nuns continued to pray and praise God and forgive those opposing them. What an example of courage and faithfulness for our times! Diocesan exorcism team member Kathleen Beckman drives home this important point:

> It's time to be braver in driving out sin and evil in our families, so that our homes can be demon-free zones. St. Catherine of Siena teaches: "Start being brave about everything. Drive out the darkness and spread light. Don't look at your weaknesses. Realize instead that in Christ crucified you can do everything."[60]

The Miraculous Statue

First, a word about the Catholic perspective on the difference between worship and veneration. The first commandment calls us to worship God and no one else (see CCC 2083, 2135). The Church calls this *latria* — worship belongs to God alone. However, the Church honors angels, saints, and relics in a subordinate way because of their special relationship to God.[61] We call this veneration *dulia*. Veneration of Mary is special since her role as *Theotokos*, or "God-bearer," is unique. We call her veneration *hyperdulia*. Therefore, the Church distinguishes between the worship due to God alone and the honor we bestow on Mary and the other saints. As a part of showing this honor and respect, we have statues of Our Lady, angels, and saints. But we do not worship these representations of holy persons or angelic beings. These statues remind us of the goodness and protection of Our Lord through His Church triumphant in Heaven.

Our Lady asked Mother Mariana to build a statue of herself under the title of Our Lady of Good Success of the Purification, referring to the presentation of the Child Jesus in the temple. Our Lady's request came on January 16, 1599, when Mother was in prison. Our Lady spoke to Mother:

> I am Mary of Good Success, your Mother in Heaven, to whom you always have recourse with this invocation known in Spain.... The tribulation whereby today my Blessed Son tries you is a Heavenly gift with which souls fortify themselves and hold back the Divine wrath.[62]

In addition to offering her sufferings for the horrendous sins being committed in the colony, Mother instilled in her sisters a great love for their divine vocation per Our Lady's request. In the midst of an ungrateful and perverse world, Our Lady promised that there would always be holy sisters obtaining tremendous blessings for the Church,

Ecuador, and souls. In fact, Our Lady prophesized to Mother that the colony would become a free republic and be named Ecuador.

As many public and private calamites would beset the region, the sisters' role as powerful intercessors would become even more important.[63] Anyone reading the history of Ecuador from that period onward can see how many disasters, revolts, turmoil, and divisions roiled that region. And yet, Our Lady's promise of great protection must have been a strong encouragement during the diabolical trials that threatened to destroy the convent. The Gospels reveal the nature of our enemy: "He was a murderer from the beginning, and has nothing to do with the truth, because there is no truth in him. When he lies, he speaks according to his own nature, for he is a liar and the father of lies" (John 8:44).

Our Lady also revealed that secret societies would infiltrate civil government and cause cruel persecutions of religious communities, especially the Conceptionist convent in Quito. However, God would triumph and prevent attempts to close the convent through the centuries.

Let us return to the miraculous statue commissioned by Our Lady, which was the will of her Divine Son. This statue would be the concrete representation of Mary's authority over the convent. Our Lady gave several hopeful counsels to Mother Mariana during this apparition.[64] Mary requested that the statue be placed above the abbess's seat as a reminder of her role as the heavenly abbess.

At first, Mother felt incompetent for the task because she did not think that any person could capture Our Lady's beauty or her exact height in order to tell the artist. Our Lady gave her the name of an artist — Francisco del Castillo — to begin the project. Besides being deeply pious, Francisco's gifted hand was impaired. The Virgin asked Mother to take measurements of her using her cincture, the Franciscan cord that the Conceptionists wear around their waist. Our Lady told Mother to give her one end of the cord and bring the other end to her foot. Although the cord was too short, the Infant Jesus held the other end given to Him by His Mother. The cord stretched miraculously to reach Our Lady's forehead.

Mother Mariana needed permission from Bishop Salvador de Ribera before starting the project. Thinking the bishop would say no, she put off having the statue made. Matthew Arnold writes:

> Mother Mariana was afraid that Bishop Ribera would not believe that Mary had really spoken to her, and so she hesitated. To make a long story short, ten years went by without Mother Mariana acting on Our Lady's request.[65]

In another apparition, Our Lady gently admonished Mother for delaying the making of the statue. Mother Mariana was sorry and explained a new concern: she was afraid that the newly evangelized native people — who tended toward idolatry — would get the wrong idea about the statue. Mother wanted to keep them from this error. The bishop unexpectedly supported the statue. He even told Mother that she should have contacted him sooner. He also asked her to make a request from Our Lady. Namely, the bishop sought to extend his life beyond the period indicated in the prophecy to Mother.[66] The prophecy had stated that the bishop would live two more years.

The most amazing part of the miraculous statue is how it was completed. When the artist Francisco del Castillo was finishing his final touches on the statue, he left for Europe to purchase some special paints for the face. On January 21, 1610, the day before Francisco returned with his special paints, Arnold writes:

> Mother Mariana was at prayer in the upper choir near midnight, as was her custom, when she beheld a vision of the Holy Trinity in the Tabernacle. She also saw the three Archangels — Michael, Gabriel and Raphael — kneeling before the Divine Majesty.[67]

Then she saw St. Francis directing the angels in the upper choir as they miraculously completed the statue of Our Lady with the Child Jesus. Upon completion, St. Francis placed his white cord around the waist of the statue. Then Our Lady entered into the statue, and it "took on life and intoned with the celestial choir the *Magnificat*."[68] The sisters were awakened by the heavenly music and came to the choir; they saw a brilliant light that overshadowed the marvelously transformed statue.[69] When the artist returned the next day, he was astonished at the statue's beauty, attributing it to the work of Heaven. The bishop was also amazed at the final product. Both the bishop and the sculptor documented the miracle for the convent archives.

While Our Lady was working miracles inside the convent walls, she was also concerned with Catholics living in the world, especially the leaders of nations, as will be seen in the next chapter.

CHAPTER FOUR

A Truly Devout Catholic President

The Prophecy Concerning the President on January 16, 1599

OUR LADY GAVE THE following prophecy to Mother concerning a future Catholic president of Ecuador, whose authentic character and noble leadership would win heaven's acclaim:

> In the nineteenth century a truly Christian president will come, a man of character to whom God Our Lord will grant the palm of martyrdom in this very square where my convent is. He will consecrate the republic to the Sacred Heart of my beloved Son, and this consecration will sustain the Catholic religion throughout the following years. During those years, which will be ominous for the Church, the accursed sect of Freemasonry will take over the civil government. A cruel persecution will rage against all religious communities and will descend upon this convent with special fury. Because of those wretched men the convent would perish, but God lives and I live and We will raise powerful defenders from their own midst. We shall place insuperable difficulties in their path; the triumph will be Ours.[70]

The Fulfillment

Don Gabriel Garcia Moreno loved God and his countrymen. He acted boldly and possessed a deep passion for the truth. While in political exile in Paris, he once studied for sixteen hours a day to learn the best form of government and educational system for his nation, almost ruining his health in the process. His zeal to learn the truth was a self-imposed duty that he embraced wholeheartedly.

Writer Maxwell-Scott wrote of his parents that "both were devout and amiable."[71] Moreno initially studied for the priesthood at the University in Quito but later changed to law after discernment. He was a devout Catholic for most of his life. After his lengthy studies in Paris, he realized that only the Catholic Faith could save and unify Ecuador, which was rife with divisions and revolts. Moreno understood that a nation without religion would fall prey to autocrats or anarchists.[72] Unfortunately, autocrats and anarchists played a large role in his country before he became president.

President Moreno's daily schedule reflected his Catholic values in a clear and unapologetic way. He started his day at 5:00 a.m. with meditation followed by daily Mass at 6:00 a.m. At 7:00 a.m., he visited the sick at the hospital and then afterward worked diligently in his library until 10:00 a.m. After eating a frugal breakfast, he went to the Government Palace until 3:00 p.m. He dined at 4:00 p.m. and made necessary visits, public works inspections, and settled disputes before returning home to be with his family until 9:00 p.m. Next, he would return to his library to write letters and work until 11:00 p.m. or midnight.[73] Within his busy schedule, the vivacious president also prayed the daily Rosary, which along with his other faith commitments, became his Catholic compass throughout the day. Let us look at President Moreno's early life.

Garcia Moreno was born on Christmas Eve in 1821 in Guayaquil, a hot and humid Pacific coastal port city. Garcia was the youngest of four brothers and three sisters. Don Gabriel Garcia Gomez, his father's name, was given to him at Baptism.[74] His father was a strong Catholic and had contempt for the Liberals of that time, who wanted to free themselves from Spain and religion.[75] His mother, Dona Mercedes Moreno, possessed great faith and virtue, and so young Garcia had tremendous examples to imitate.

When he was young, Garcia was timid and somewhat fearful — the exact opposite of the boldness that later became a hallmark of his character. Therefore, his father sought to instill courage in his son. To face the fear of storms, he locked him at night on the balcony during a severe thunderstorm. On another occasion, he had him light his candle near a dead body and stay in the room to overcome his fear of death. Although we might use different means today, both actions were successful.[76] Later in life, we find Garcia conquering other fears as an explorer and soldier.

The Moreno family instilled the Catholic Faith in all their children. Fr. Augustine Berthe, who published a comprehensive book on Garcia Moreno shortly after his death, said of the remarkable Moreno family that Garcia drew "lively faith, chivalrous honor and especially that noble passion for duty" from them.[77] The family members served in various vocations, including the priesthood, government, and business.

Unfortunately, due to numerous revolutions in South America at the time and other factors, his father's business failed, and the family became impoverished. To make matters worse, his father died unexpectedly. Thankfully, all of his older siblings were educated professionals before his father passed away. So his mother home-schooled Garcia until a priest friend, Fr. Miguel Betancourt, seeing the family troubles, offered to tutor him in Latin and other subjects. The kindly monk was amazed that Garcia mastered Latin and the other subjects in ten months. Fr. Betancourt was then able to secure room and board through relatives for fifteen-year-old Garcia to attend the University of Quito. The young man, with a passion for justice, worked hard at his studies because he was grateful for this educational opportunity.

Garcia Moreno adopted a motto for his political view: *Liberty for everyone and everything except for evil and evildoers.* Incorporating this motto into his practice of law, he would not take any bad or suspect cases. Fr. Berthe explained: "On one occasion the presiding judge, having asked him to undertake the defense of a notorious assassin, he refused point-blank, with the exclamation: 'It would be easier for me to become a murderer than to defend one!' "[78] Yet he always helped the poor clients *pro bono*. But his ultimate calling involved national politics.

Garcia had flaws like every good man. While exiled, he became somewhat lax in going regularly to Confession. After being challenged by a friend for his nominal faith, he reverted to his ardent Catholic practices. And when he was impatient, he learned to admit his fault and make it right. As the saints, too, had to overcome faults, Garcia Moreno was no exception to that rule.

In 1848, he married Dona Rosa Ascusabi, who came from nobility. Maxwell-Scott describes her and the marriage in this way: "She was clever and charming, and their union was one of great happiness, saddened only by the storms of public life and the many separations which Moreno's duties rendered necessary."[79]

The two shared much in common as, writes Fr. Berthe, she was "of a nature in entire conformity with the ideas and character of her husband."[80] The substantial political upheaval in Ecuador, however, proved challenging for Dona Rosa, and rightly so.

Ecuador was marked by revolutions, anarchy, and instability from the time Garcia Moreno was very young. Heavy-handed dictators looking out for their own gain at the expense of the people, anti-Catholic radicals trying to suppress the Church, corruption and graft — stealing a portion of the revenues — created a series of storms and chaos. In this milieu, Garcia Moreno led soldiers and worked as a journalist to expose the rogues ruling the country until he was forced into exile by these same tyrants for his hard-hitting writing. He once wrote of Ecuador's leader, José María Urbina: "No vice, no crime, is unknown to him. Treason, perjury, swindling, brigandage, savage cruelty, perfidy, nothing is wanting. His ignoble life is written bit by bit in the penal code."[81] Garcia's stalwart character kept him in the fight for a stable and free Ecuador.

After almost thirty years of bloody revolution and anarchy in Ecuador, with its terrible toll on the country, Garcia Moreno became president. He had earned the respect of many in his battle against the tyrants. Fr. Berthe highlights the moment:

> During the last fifteen years, we have admired Garcia Moreno as a patriot and head of the Opposition, determined to deliver his country from the tyrants who oppressed her. We have now to follow him in his government of the country he had saved.[82]

Garcia Moreno wasted no time in confronting the serious problems that had developed in the country.

The Major Reforms

In a systematic manner, President Moreno began a series of sweeping reforms that saved the country from ruin. These major reforms centered on the following: the economy, the military, education, and establishing Ecuador's relationship to the Holy See. President Moreno also recognized the great benefit of infrastructure, particularly roadways. But first, he had to reform the entire electoral system because it was unjust and not based on the actual population.

Under Spain, Ecuador was divided into three large districts: Quito, Cuenca, and Guayaquil. Each would send ten deputies to the Convention. Therefore, Guayaquil and Cuenca could checkmate the Quito deputies, who were mainly conservatives and whose province had three times the population size as the other two. As a result, Catholics were almost always represented by liberal and ultra-radical politicians, who opposed the Church or wanted to destroy her.[83] Thus, President Moreno issued the following decree:

The election will be based on the numbers of the population. Each fraction of twenty thousand inhabitants will elect a deputy. The election will be direct and the suffrage (right to vote) universal. Every citizen of twenty years of age who can read and write will be qualified to vote.[84]

In addition to reforming the electoral system, he dealt with corrupt judges and the political appointment schema — the Ecuadorian swamp, if you will.

The Moreno economic reform made dramatic improvements for the treasury and the common man. President Moreno installed trustworthy public officials into positions. Writer Michael Chad Shibler reports that "previous liberal regimes had thrived upon rampant corruption," but "under Garcia Moreno's firm hand, public officials soon realized that such infractions were not tolerated."[85] President Moreno donated half of his salary to the national treasury and the other half to public charities.[86] Historian Joseph Sladky underscored how previous rogue leaders caused many serious problems in the country: "The government had borrowed with abandon, taxed the people mercilessly, failed to control spending and had not kept a budget."[87] Ecuador's credit rating was in the tank, but all of President Moreno's economic reforms began to attract foreign investment. He "introduced a better method of bookkeeping for accounting, created a Board of Control to act as a check on fraud by the executive body, and removed all officials involved in peculation."[88] The economic growth was the best under President Moreno since the republic began. Take a look at the data:

Between 1852 and 1890, Ecuador's exports grew in value from slightly more than US $1 million to nearly US $10 million. Production of cacao, the most important export product in the late nineteenth century, grew from 6.5 million kilograms to 18 million kilograms during the same period.[89]

Another priority for President Moreno was to reform the military because it had degenerated into a band of undisciplined rogues that pillaged, at times, from the rich and the poor. "An army thus constituted," he exclaimed, "is a cancer which eats out the very heart of a people. Either I will reform it or I will destroy it."[90] Since a well-trained and disciplined military was needed in a country that had experienced many revolutions and threats from neighboring countries, President Moreno attacked the problem on several levels. Frank Rega explained that President Moreno felt a small, well-equipped military and a larger fully trained national guard for special times of emergency were necessary; also, President Moreno reformed the corrupt system of recruiting and created a cadet school for training career army officers. He also provided chaplains to every regiment for the sacraments, religious instruction, and annual retreats. Furthermore, he equipped the army with the latest weapons and equipment.[91] The strong measures and firm penalties for misconduct were gradually transformative. Fr. Berthe remarked that "army discipline was once more restored, and the troops became a protection, instead of a terror, to the whole country."[92]

After this reform process was well underway, he turned his attention to education, which had fared badly under the anti-clerical dictators, Jose Flores and Jose Maria Urbina. Sadly, these dictators were more interested in power, gold, and position than in empowering the youth and society through learning.

Transforming education was a huge goal for President Moreno. He believed in universal literacy and in many French pedagogical concepts from his time in exile. To gain the best ideas for public education should he ever be elected president, he visited all the lyceums and colleges.[93] From his studies in Paris, he began to see the indispensable role of the Catholic Faith in restoring Christian civilization, especially in his country. Sladky clarifies this foundational point:

Just as the revolutionaries and freemasons wished to la-
icize education, eradicating any influence of morality and
religion on the young, he set to do just the opposite. He
invited French religious congregations to mold the minds
and hearts of the young in their schools and to care for the
sick in hospitals and the criminals in prisons. The ex-
pelled Jesuits were also recalled.[94]

The radicals were furious with Garcia Moreno, but he steadfastly
continued to expand education in his first two terms as president.
He understood the immense value of a complete education to re-
generate a nation with religion first and the human sciences second.
He focused on primary education in his first term. In his second
term, through a new education bill, he made education compulsory
for all children eight years and older.[95] Shibler offers a glimpse at
some of the numbers:

In 1873, there were approximately 8,000 children in primary schools but just two years later, thanks to Garcia
Moreno's efforts, there were over 32,000 children attending school. After six years of intensive schooling, there
was more real progress in Ecuador than had occurred in
the previous 50 years of revolutionary rule.[96]

Under his administration, Ecuador became a leader in science and
higher education within Latin America. Historian Sladky emphasized
that President Moreno believed that a country's greatness goes beyond its material progress: "Unlike many modern politicians who
measure the greatness of a civilization by its material progress, Garcia
Moreno understood that the touchstone of a true civilization is the
moral and religious perfection of its people."[97] With the Jesuits' help,
he established colleges throughout the country, giving them the
freedom to follow their traditional methods. President Moreno even
had a magnificent college built in Quito. Two hundred professors

were sent from this college to open schools throughout the country. The total enrollment of these new schools in Ecuador soon reached a thousand students.[98]

The dignity of every person was paramount for President Moreno. He established special schools for the native Indians, who were scared by the revolutionaries into the idea that conscription might follow if they educated their children. "Garcia Moreno also opened special schools for the native Indians, in spite of the dread, ... they would be liable to the conscription," Fr. Berthe pointed out.[99]

Love and respect for his countrymen was a motivating force in President Moreno's life. He once wrote:

> I am neither a ministerialist, nor a place hunter, never having chosen to sell myself for money, nor am I a soldier boasting of the blows I have given or received. I am simply the friend of an unfortunate people who have no defenders against the devils who oppress them, and I will fight to the death against those who martyrize or betray them.[100]

His 1869 constitution guaranteed equal rights for all Ecuadoreans, further proof of his respect for the sanctity of life. It established the right to innocence until proven guilty, a right to free speech and assembly, so long as it respected religion, morality, and decency, and prohibited arrests without warrants.[101]

The president's concern for the poor and marginalized was both corporal and spiritual. As Sladky writes: "He made his particular cause the well-being of the Indians and rural poor in the interior of Ecuador, sponsoring missions by the Jesuits and Redemptorists and protecting this simple people from exploitation."[102] His charitable works and other actions, such as increasing the number of hospitals staffed by nuns, were innumerable. His love for his people — especially the poor — was not mere words. He lived out everything he said.

His example of defending the most vulnerable members of his society ought to inspire every Catholic leader to protect the most innocent members of our times, the unborn and children who are sex trafficked.

Now let us turn our attention to another important achievement of the action-oriented president: building roads.

As alluded to earlier, Ecuador's lack of roads and treacherous terrain in the early nineteenth century inhibited travel. President Moreno knew that national highways and railroads would build up the nation and economy. So he initiated major roads, such as connecting Quito with Guayaquil. Although this highway took ten years to build, it is another lasting achievement of the Catholic president. Writer Gary Potter adds that a railroad was also constructed to further improve travel between the two cities: "A railroad over the mountains between Quito and Guayaquil was begun so that the two main sections of the country, the Costa and the Sierra, would be brought together."[103]

The infrastructure improvements included building lighthouses, paving streets, and the beautification of Quito.[104] These additions not only made travel and trade easier but also helped unify the revolution-torn country.

To strengthen his country's soul, "her faith life," even more so than her body, "her infrastructure," President Moreno sought assistance from Rome. In 1862, he helped establish a concordat with the Catholic Church (one of his first goals) during his first term as president. A concordat is an agreement between the pope and a government for the regulation of ecclesiastical matters. The president sent a young, well-educated priest who shared his views to represent Ecuador in negotiations with the Church. Sladky describes the view of the Church: "From the perspective of the Church, this concordat (1862) was one of the most favorable concordats ever negotiated with any State."[105] Since religious orders could be exiled and Church property could be seized by the revolutionaries without any repercussions, President Moreno sought to stop these heinous acts. He gave this instruction to his envoy:

> I wish for the complete liberty of the Church and the complete reform also of the secular and regular clergy. I entreat the Sovereign Pontiff to send us a Nuncio invested with supreme power to enforce these reforms upon all.[106]

The concordat ensured that education was based on Catholic principles, and the bishops alone would decide on all books for the human sciences, religion, and morals. The Church would have full control over her property.[107] The concordat produced tremendous fruits, including a well-ordered society with virtuous citizens.

But President Moreno was not finished helping protect the Church and the country he loved. In his second term, he did something that no Catholic president had ever done before. He consecrated Ecuador to the Sacred Heart of Jesus. Fr. Berthe traces the proposal from its beginning: "He proposed it first to the bishops at the third Council of Quito, who received the idea with enthusiasm."[108] The Congress also approved of the concept. Strong opposition was voiced by his enemies, who claimed it would destroy Ecuador. "Yet he was doing nothing less than ushering in the social Kingship of Christ — this is precisely what Pius XI outlined in *Quas Primas* over fifty years later," Sladky reminds us.[109]

Shibler underscores the scriptural basis for President Moreno's and Archbishop Checa y Barba's act:

> "Seek ye first the kingdom of Heaven and all other things will be given to thee." He achieved his audacious goals by ordering all things according to the will of the Sacred Heart of Jesus. He believed, as does the Church, that any civil society that does not acknowledge the King of Heaven cannot truly progress.[110]

Civil and ecclesiastical leaders joined President Moreno and Archbishop Checa y Barba on that special day. The solemn ceremony occurred at the cathedral. Trumpets sounded, rifles fired, and church bells rang in unison throughout Ecuador. For the first time in history, a Republic was consecrated to the Sacred Heart of Jesus.[111] This unforgettable day would endure in the collective memory of the Ecuadoreans for centuries, even being passed onto future generations.

The Martyrdom of a Great President

They say every big ship makes waves, but that is especially true when that big ship is Catholic and recognizes Jesus Christ's kingship over the nation. President Moreno was no small ship. Guided by the Holy Spirit, Ecuador flourished under his command because respect and service were greatly prized. After his third term landslide victory in May 1875, warnings of assassination began to creep in. For months, these threats surfaced. Friends urged him to take extra precautions, such as having an escort of guards. President Moreno wrote back:

> I am very grateful for your charitable advice, though it tells me nothing new. I know very well that certain men wish for my death; but these wishes only injure those who form them. Tell the person who gave you the warning that I fear God, but God alone. I forgive my enemies with all my heart; I would do good to them if I knew who they were, and if they gave me the opportunity.[112]

Revolutionaries from secret societies in neighboring countries, instigated by Germany, were determined to overthrow the government. The president explained: "I am warned from Germany ... that the Lodges of that country have given orders to those of America to move heaven and earth to overthrow the government of Ecuador. But if God protects and overshadows us by His mercy, what have we to fear?"[113]

Don Gabriel Garcia Moreno had overcome his timidity as a youngster and by faith understood his destiny was in the hands of God.

He knew his days were numbered. He wrote to Pope Pius IX, seeking his prayers for divine protection and to let him know that he was happy to die a martyr for Christ. On August 4, 1875, President Moreno wrote to his close friend from college, Juan Aguirre, who was in Europe at the time, to wish him a final good-bye. "*Adios!* We shall never meet again on earth.... I am about to be assassinated but I am happy to die for my faith."[114]

The plot to murder President Moreno took on flesh as Faustino Rayo, "who held a grudge against Moreno for dismissing him from a lucrative office because of his dishonest practices,"[115] and his radical associates began to shadow him. Rayo pretended to be Moreno's friend, and the president even contracted with him to make a saddle for his young son.[116]

On First Friday, August 6, 1875, President Moreno went into the cathedral to adore the Blessed Sacrament. The cathedral is located in the same Santo Domingo Plaza where the Conceptionist convent stands, where Mother Mariana lived nearly three hundred years before.

Shibler informs us of the assassins' next move as they waited in the plaza for Moreno: "The assassins, noting that he was spending a long time in prayer, sent a messenger into the church to call him out. Seemingly oblivious to the mortal danger, Garcia Moreno had only one aide-de-camp with him."[117] After receiving the message, the president departed from the cathedral and started toward the adjacent Presidential Palace.

As he approached the entrance, Rayo suddenly attacked the president with his machete. His fellow assassins fired their revolvers but only grazed him. Rayo struck multiple times and screamed, "Die, destroyer of liberty!" President Moreno spoke as he lay dying, "God does not die!" Marian Horvat relates that "these were the last words of a line he often repeated, 'I am only a man who can be killed and replaced, but God does not die.'"[118]

In the mayhem, some thought a revolution was happening. A young man jumped on Rayo to stop his attack but was injured and repelled. Moreno's aid ran to the barracks for help. People rapidly filled the square. Soldiers scrambled to find the murderers. Priests from the cathedral rushed out to give aid to the dying president. Finally, he was carried into the cathedral and a priest asked him if he forgave his murderers; his facial gestures indicated that he had done so. The Sacrament of Extreme Unction was given to the fallen hero.[119]

Rayo had taken a bullet in the leg that was meant for the president and so could not escape as fast as the other assassins. The self-deceived Rayo brandished his weapon as if to provoke a demonstration. One of the soldiers aimed directly at him as Rayo yelled, "You have no right to kill me!" and the angry reply he received was: "And you, what right had you to assassinate my master?" The first assassin was shot dead on the spot as the manhunt continued for the others.[120] Authorities discovered a large amount of Peruvian currency — payment for the hit. Horvat relayed that "the crowds took [the murderer's] body, dragging it through the streets, and left it unburied for the vultures to feed upon."[121] Such was the anger and sorrow of the Ecuadorian citizens after their great president was assassinated.

Quito turned into a place of immense mourning. Sladky reports:

> The whole town of Quito went into mourning, with the bells tolling continuously. The conspirators thought that the assassination would break into a revolution. They were to be disappointed. For three days, while his body lay in State in the Cathedral, thousands of sobbing people came to pay their respects to the man who had done so much for their country. In the session of 16 September

1875, the Ecuadorian Congress issued a decree in which
they paid homage to Garcia Moreno as "The Regenerator
of his country, and the Martyr of Catholic Civilization."[122]

Pope Pius IX paid Gabriel Garcia Moreno tremendous honor by
referring to him as a man who died "the death of a martyr ... a victim
to his Faith and Christian charity." He is considered one of the greatest Catholic statesmen in the modern era. His incorrupt heart is on
display in the Cathedral of Quito, a sign of his burning love for the
Sacred Heart.[123]

Thus the prophecy of Our Lady of Good Success of the Purification regarding Gabriel Garcia Moreno, the great Catholic president of the nineteenth century, was fulfilled. Let us look at some of
the prophecies concerning the modern epoch and the twentieth
century.

CHAPTER FIVE

Prophecies Concerning
the Modern Epoch

Struggles against Doubt

TEN YEARS AFTER THE Virgin asked Mother to carve a statue of Our Lady of Good Success of the Purification, Mother still had not fulfilled her request. Mother still had doubts about the apparitions, a common experience for some visionaries. As alluded to previously, Mother also worried that the simple people of the colony would make an idol out of the statue.

Praying in the early morning of January 21, 1610, Mother suddenly felt a deep joy and love within. The archangels St. Gabriel, St. Michael, and St. Raphael appeared. Each archangel uniquely addressed her as a privileged daughter and indicated that the Mother of God would soon visit. All three archangels imparted different spiritual gifts to Mother and exhorted her to not doubt the apparitions. Finally, they strengthened and healed Mother. Mother Mariana thanked the heavenly messengers for their light and praised God that He was so good to the least of all His creatures.

After the archangels departed, Our Lady arrived, calling Mother Mariana her favored daughter and beloved spouse of my Divine Child. The Blessed Mother did not come alone; she appeared with her Divine Child in her left arm and crosier in her right as in past apparitions. The Virgin explained her role as Mother, her and her Son's love for souls, predicted the multitude of faithful and unfaithful religious who will live in the convent through the centuries, and explained how they are assisted with the Eucharist to help them reach Heaven. The Virgin said, however, that the faithful and unfaithful both have free will and can use it to choose the path to Heaven or to Hell. She also spoke of the heroic souls who would win many graces for our sinful world.[124] Then the Virgin prophesized a serious Church and world crisis that would emerge at the end of the nineteenth century and shortly after the middle of the twentieth century. This crisis would coincide with the start of the sexual revolution in the twentieth century. Let us examine this prophecy in parts.

The Great Crisis

Our Lady of Good Success declared the following:

> Thus I make it known to you that from the end of the 19th century and from shortly after the middle of the 20th century, in what is today the Colony and will then be the Republic of Ecuador, the passions will erupt and there will be a total corruption of customs, for Satan will reign almost completely by means of the Masonic sects.

> They will focus principally on the children in order to sustain this general corruption. Woe to the children of these times! It will be difficult to receive the Sacrament of Baptism, and also that of Confirmation. They will receive the Sacrament of Confession only if they remain in Catholic schools, for the Devil will make a great effort to destroy it through persons in positions of authority.

> The same thing will happen with Holy Communion. Alas! How deeply I grieve to manifest to you the many enormous sacrileges — both public as well as secret — that will occur from profanations of the Holy Eucharist. Often during this epoch the enemies of Jesus Christ, instigated by the Devil, will steal consecrated hosts from the churches so that they might profane the Eucharistic

Species. My Most Holy Son will see Himself cast upon the ground and trampled upon by filthy feet.[125]

We already cited how an American Satanist claimed to have consecrated Hosts and planned to use them in a public black mass. Thankfully, an archbishop filed a lawsuit and stopped this sacrilege and profanation of the Holy Eucharist. Consecrated Hosts are being stolen more frequently by Satanists, sometimes in a very public manner. Meanwhile, fewer Catholics are receiving the sacraments.

In a large Midwestern diocese, Dr. Ralph Martin points out that from 2000 to 2010, the number of infant baptisms declined 42.4 percent, and adult baptisms declined in the same period 51.2 percent. Statistics from other dioceses, including those in the Catholic heartland, are very similar.[126] Unbaptized souls are deprived of so many graces, especially sanctifying grace, the very life of God. Many nominal Catholics do not grasp the importance of Baptism, Confirmation, and Confession; therefore, they neglect to provide their children with these sacraments and the corresponding graces that greatly aid Christian living. Sadly, some in positions of authority also do not recognize the crucial importance of the sacraments. And so, Our Lady called upon Mother Mariana and her handmaidens to intercede for the world with greater urgency:

> But this convent will conserve faithful souls, devoted and fervent spouses who will make amends to Him with loving tenderness, suffering to seeing Him thus hated by their ungrateful brethren, sinners whose hearts will hardly seem to be human. They will pray for these sinners and make great penances of every type; some will also carry the heavy cross of infirmity by which God purifies His chosen souls, and with it they will make amends for so many crimes and sacrileges committed in the world. The wily demon will try to impede this, placing in the imaginations of my suffering

daughters ideas of despair with the intent of making them lose the merit they have gained.

But in those times you will already be known, as well as the favors that I am bestowing on you. How I love the fortunate inhabitants of this sacred place! And that knowledge will stimulate love and devotion to my Sacred Statue. For this reason, today I authoritatively order you to have this statue made: Let it be sculpted just as you see me and placed upon the abbess' chair, so that from there I may govern and direct my daughters and defend my convent; for Satan, making use of both the good and the evil, will engage in a fierce battle to destroy it.

This battle will reach its most acute stage because some irresponsible religious, under the appearance of virtue and with bad-intentioned zeal, will undermine the existence of their Mother — the religious life — who nourished them at her breast. These souls will assume massive responsibility for their actions. Only by Divine Mercy will they arrive at purgatory to be purified by its fires.

All these souls should tremble upon learning of this future destiny! Falling into themselves, they must struggle to reform their convent, reforming themselves first. Above all, they must have a heroic charity, carefully and lovingly guarding in their hearts the weaknesses they discover in their sisters. Without this divine charity not a single virtue can exist, for charity and profound humility are the only solid foundation of religious perfection. Without them, there can only be a simulation of virtue that barely covers the putrefaction of the soul.[127]

Our Lady's message focuses on the internal life of the convent, but especially the necessity of ongoing conversion and vigilance to thwart the evil one. Even though Mary's role has been downplayed by some in the Church, a Marian springtime is happening throughout the world. Thanks to great saints like Pope St. John Paul II, many souls are now consecrating their lives to the Blessed Mother.

The Virgin also reminded Mother Mariana that charity and humility are the cornerstones of holiness and the key to growth in virtue, especially in religious life.

Our Lady further lamented the utter neglect and disdain for the sacraments to Mother Mariana:

> Since this poor country will lack the Catholic spirit, the Sacrament of Extreme Unction will be little valued. Many people will die without receiving it, either because of the negligence of their families or a misconceived affection for their sick ones. Others, incited by the cursed Devil, will rebel against the spirit of the Catholic Church and will deprive countless souls of innumerable graces, consolations and the strength they need to make that great leap from time to eternity. But some persons will die without receiving it due to just and secret chastisements of God.
>
> As for the Sacrament of Matrimony, which symbolizes the union of Christ with His Church, it will be attacked and deeply profaned. Freemasonry, which will then be in power, will enact iniquitous laws with the aim of doing away with this sacrament, making it easy for everyone to live in sin and encouraging the procreation of illegitimate children born without the blessing of the Church. The Catholic spirit will rapidly decay; the precious light of Faith will gradually be extinguished until there will be an almost total and general corruption of customs. Added to this will be the effects of secular education, which will be one reason for the death of priestly and religious vocations.[128]

Cardinal Carlo Caffarra was commissioned by Pope St. John Paul II to establish the Pontifical Institute for Studies on Marriage and Family.

The Institute was entrusted in a special way to Our Lady of Fatima. At the onset of the project, the cardinal wrote to Sr. Lucia, the oldest Fatima seer, to ask for her prayers. Sr. Lucia replied in a letter that is now in the archives:

> The final battle between the Lord and the kingdom of Satan will be about Marriage and the Family. Do not be afraid, because whoever works for the sanctity of Marriage and the Family will always be fought against and opposed in every way, because this is the decisive issue.[129]

Since God is a family of three persons, it makes perfect sense that Satan would attack the human family, the very representation of the Blessed Trinity on earth. In *Familiaris Consortio*, John Paul II wrote:

> All that you succeed in doing to support the family is destined to have an effectiveness that goes beyond its own sphere and reaches other people too, and has an effect on society. The future of the world and of the Church passes through the family.[130]

Commenting on the prophecy's reference to the attack on the Sacrament of Matrimony, Matthew Arnold writes:

> The staggering amount of co-habitation, Catholic marriages that end in divorce, and the Supreme Court decision in favor of so-called "gay marriage" makes it quite clear that this prophecy has come true.[131]

Regarding the part of the message that discusses the plight of children, Arnold highlights that "since 1965, a 50% decrease in US Catholic weddings has been accompanied by a 50% decrease in infant baptisms."[132] Fortunately, the Church has remedies for couples and children seeking to be in full communion.

Besides neglecting the Sacraments of Marriage and Baptism, many Catholics no longer value the Sacrament of the Anointing of the Sick, or Extreme Unction. The latter sacrament offers tremendous physical and spiritual healing. Some neglect this sacrament out of a false compassion for sick family members or because they think this sacrament will scare their relative by raising the issue of imminent death. And yet, facilitating this sacrament is true compassion. It requires thinking of a person's eternal good and even temporal good, who may obtain physical healing through the encounter with Christ in the sacrament.

Our Lady of Good Success predicted additional attacks on other sacraments:

> The Sacrament of Holy Orders will be ridiculed, oppressed and despised, for in this sacrament, the Church of God and even God Himself is scorned and despised since He is represented in His priests. The Devil will try to persecute the ministers of the Lord in every possible way; he will labor with cruel and subtle astuteness to deviate them from the spirit of their vocation and will corrupt many of them. These depraved priests, who will scandalize the Christian people, will make the hatred of bad Catholics and the enemies of the Roman Catholic and Apostolic Church fall upon all priests.
>
> This apparent triumph of Satan will bring enormous sufferings to the good pastors of the Church, the many good priests, and the supreme pastor and Vicar of Christ on earth, who, a prisoner in the Vatican, will shed secret and bitter tears in the presence of his God and Lord, beseeching light, sanctity and perfection for all the clergy of the world, of whom he is King and Father.
>
> Further, in these unhappy times, there will be unbridled luxury that will ensnare the rest into sin and conquer

innumerable frivolous souls who will be lost. Innocence will almost no longer be found in children, nor modesty in women. In this supreme moment of need of the Church, the one who should speak will fall silent.[133]

Our Lady's prophecy regarding corrupt priests was given over four hundred years ago, yet it sounds like she spoke it yesterday. The clergy abuse scandals have caused many to express their hatred toward all priests to the point of verbal and even physical abuse. The inability to discriminate between bad actors (only a small percentage of priests are corrupt) and the many faithful priests who are living their vocation is unfortunately all too common today. Yes, throwing every bishop or priest under the bus is following the bad example of the enemies of the Church. Still, a zero-tolerance policy is needed along with criminal prosecution for the guilty parties. Often, we see this blanket condemnation of priests and bishops on social media platforms because of the actions or statements of a few.

There is a famous quote that says that all that is necessary for the triumph of evil is that good men do nothing. They not only do nothing, but they also remain quiet. Our Lady echoed these sentiments, "In this supreme moment of need of the Church, the one who should speak will fall silent." Dr. Ralph Martin addresses this troubling silence:

> Today there is quite a remarkable silence regarding the areas of the truth revealed by God that are most in conflict with our culture. Hardly ever is there a clear sermon on the seriousness of sexual sin, where the sins are actually specified. Scarcely ever is there a sermon on the eternal consequences of not repenting from serious sin, not just sexual sin, but all kinds of sins.... Almost never is there excommunication for so-called "practicing Catholics" who boldly and publicly deny there is any contradiction

between aggressively supporting abortion and same-sex relationships and claiming to be a good Catholic.[134]

Let us remember the powerful words of a great saint and doctor of the Church, St. Catherine of Siena: "We've had enough exhortations to be silent. Cry out with a thousand tongues — I see the world is rotten because of silence." It is time for the disturbing silence to end, because speaking the truth in love brings life, and ignoring issues causes spiritual death!

Besides silence on pressing moral issues by Church leaders, Our Lady addresses another major burning problem facing the world: the assault on children's innocence. Sex education programs and internet pornography have tainted children. Matthew Arnold, commenting on this prophecy, stated:

> You have only to turn on the radio, TV or the Internet to see how the innocence of children is under constant assault, not to mention outrageous public school "sex education" programs. Immodest dress (especially for girls), sexual innuendo, violence, crude humor and disrespect for parental authority are all common fare dished up daily through the modern media in materials marketed directly to children.[135]

Bear in mind that Our Lady gave her messages when the world was purer. Hence her messages might have seemed unimaginable to Mother Mariana, but not to people of our times. Sadly, impurity and immodesty are so widespread and yet rarely even addressed.

Our Lady had other important messages for Mother Mariana, which would occur during the last years of Mother's life.

CHAPTER SIX

More Prophecies Concerning the Modern Epoch

Prophecy on February 2, 1634

MOTHER MARIANA RECEIVED MANY prophecies about her life and future events. As seen earlier, some of the events were related to the convent, the future sisters of the convent, the future events of Ecuador, and the great crisis of the Church and the world in our times. We will reflect on some of Our Lady's final prophecies to Mother.

After praying in the upper choir in the early morning of February 2, 1634, Mother Mariana noticed the sanctuary lamp had burned out. As she went to relight the lamp, Our Lady appeared with the Divine Infant and told Mother the good news of her soon entrance into the heavenly Kingdom. Our Lady also reminded Mother of her maternal love and protection for the Conceptionist Order. Then Our Lady revealed the multiple meanings of the sanctuary lamp going out:

> The first is that toward the end of the 19th century and throughout a great part of the 20th, many heresies will be propagated in these lands, which will then be a free republic. With these heresies in control, the precious light of faith will be extinguished in souls because of an almost total corruption of customs. In those times there will be great calamities, both physical and moral, public and private. The few souls who remain faithful to grace will suffer a cruel, unspeakable and prolonged martyrdom. Many of them will descend to their graves due to the violence of

suffering and will be counted among the martyrs who sacrificed themselves for the Church and the country.

Secondly, my community, which will be reduced to a small number, will be submerged in a depthless sea of unspeakable troubles. Many true vocations will perish through a lack of good judgment and prudence concerning their formation by the mistresses of novices, who should be prayerful souls well-versed in the ways of spiritual guidance but who will allow many innocent novices, after having been in the secure haven of this blessed convent, to return to the Babylon of the world to become agents of evil for the corruption of souls.

Thirdly, the lamp was extinguished because of the poisoned atmosphere of impurity that will reign at that time like a filthy sea. It will flow through the streets, squares and public places with such an astonishing lack of restraint that there will be almost no virgin souls left in the world. It is well-known that the vice of impurity extinguishes the light of faith.

The fourth meaning concerns the power of sects and their ability to penetrate homes and families, thus destroying the beauty of innocence in the hearts of children. In this way, vocations to the priesthood will diminish. In the regular clergy, because of the observance of the rule and the practice of the virtues, there will be no lack of holy priests; not so with the secular clergy, who will become attached to wealth and riches rather than their priestly ministry. How the Church will suffer during this dark night! Lacking a prelate and father to guide them with paternal love, gentleness, strength, wisdom and prudence, many priests will lose their spirit, placing their souls in great danger. Therefore, clamor insistently without tiring and weep with bitter tears in the privacy of your heart, imploring our Heavenly Father for the love of the Eucharistic Heart of my Most Holy Son to put an end to these ominous times by sending to this Church the prelate who will restore the spirit of her priests. We shall endow this dear son of mine with a rare capacity, a humility of heart, a docility to divine inspiration, the strength to defend the rights of the Church, and a tender and compassionate heart, so that, like another Christ, he will assist the great and the small, without despising the less fortunate who ask him for light and counsel in their doubts and hardships. Into his hand the scale of the sanctuary will be placed so that all may be carried out in due measure and that God be glorified. However, the lukewarmness of souls consecrated to God in the priestly and religious states will tip the scales in the opposite direction, thus allowing the cursed Satan to take possession of this land. He will achieve his victories by means of foreign and faithless people so numerous that, like a black cloud, he will darken the pure heavens of the then republic consecrated to the Sacred Heart of my Divine Son.

With these people every type of vice will enter, calling down, in turn, every kind of chastisement, such as plagues, famines, internal fighting, external disputes with other nations and apostasy, the cause of perdition of so many souls so dear to Jesus Christ and to me. In order to dissipate this black cloud, which impedes the Church from enjoying the clear day of liberty, there will be a formidable and frightful war, in which both native and foreign blood will flow, including that of secular and regular priests and other religious. This night will be most horrible, for, humanly speaking, evil will seem to have triumphed. This will mark the arrival of my hour, when I, in a marvelous way, will dethrone the proud and cursed Satan, trampling him under my heel and chaining him in the infernal abyss, finally freeing the Church and the country from his cruel tyranny.

The fifth motive for the extinguishing of the lamp is the negligence and carelessness of those possessing great wealth who will indifferently stand by and witness the oppression of the Church, the persecution of virtue and the triumph of evil without applying their riches in a holy way for the destruction of evil and the restoration of the Faith.[136]

A Plague of Heresies

This prophecy has many layers for reflection. We shall endeavor to bring light on some of the key passages. Our Lady continued to warn Mother about heresies, which have spread like wildfire in our times. Many books today promote false belief systems, which are essentially repackaged ancient pagan practices. For example, some of the destructive elements in the ancient Roman belief system led to gruesome practices in that era. Roman law and religion saw nothing wrong with infanticide. Often, they left newborns to die from exposure or as food for wild animals outside the city walls. The law allowed infants who were deformed, sickly, unwanted, and of the wrong sex to be destroyed in this manner. The Christian belief that every individual has intrinsic worth and value — made in the image of God — was foreign to the Romans. For these pagans, only the State or tribe had value. So the early Christians would rescue those babies left outside the wall on garbage piles.[137]

The Romans did not have the Ten Commandments but developed their own self-centered moral code based on the false idea that only the collective had value. Furthermore, the Romans did not have the Hebrew Scriptures and Tradition, which declared that every person was made in the image and likeness of God. Austin Ruse details some of the fruits of their other obsessions:

> The ancients were also obsessed with sex. In her book *Paul Among the People*, Sarah Ruden provides a gruesome account of the porn-saturated world of the ancient Romans.... Indeed, pornographic images were part of the

warp and woof of ancient life. These images adorned the walls of homes throughout Rome. The male need for sex was called the "necessity." The male had free reign for sexual gratification from slaves, single women and boys....There were pornographic parades throughout Rome. Parents had to have their young sons guarded on their way to and from school so they would not be kidnapped and raped.[138]

Before he became pope, Cardinal Ratzinger said orthodoxy leads to orthopraxy, or right doctrines lead to right living.[139] Adhering to false beliefs, like in ancient Rome, has real consequences. In Rome, it meant painful death for the unwanted — the vulnerable and weaker members of society.

Furthermore, in his book *Under Siege – No Finer Time to Be a Faithful Catholic*, Austin Ruse documents several popular and bizarre belief systems that many adopt today. Some offer therapy, such as an "Energy Flow Formula" in which "an energy practitioner hovers his hands over stressed-out clients in what a *Wall Street Journal* article correctly describes as a 'spa version of an exorcism.'" The charge is upwards of $2,500 for an individual session.[140]

Many of these ideologies do not point to God; rather, they focus on the self, or even lord over people and circumstances. Christianity calls us to lead others to Christ by transforming the world through grace and virtue. Heaven is our true homeland, not this passing world. Indeed, the Catholic Church invented hospitals to care for the sick.

Calamities

When most people hear the term *calamity*, they think of an earthquake or flood — that is, a disastrous event that leads to terrible loss. And yet, when abortion was legalized in many countries throughout the world, the greatest disaster resulted, which was the slaughtering of millions of innocent children. As a result, humans have become commodities, leading to other serious sins like human trafficking. Our Lady's prophecy also referenced public and private calamities in our era. Certainly, two principal calamities are human trafficking and abortion, and many believe that they have and continue to spawn ongoing violence in all sectors of our culture. Several popes and leaders have called for the end of these evils, which seek to destroy our culture. St. Teresa of Calcutta said at the February 1997 National Prayer Breakfast in Washington: "What is taking place in America is a war against the child. And if we accept that the mother can kill her own child, how can we tell other people not to kill one another." St. Teresa practiced what she preached and stated:

> Please don't kill the child. I want the child. Please give me the child. I am willing to accept any child who would be aborted, and to give that child to a married couple who will love the child, and be loved by the child. From our children's home in Calcutta alone, we have saved over 3,000 children from abortions. These children have brought such love and joy to their adoptive parents, and have grown up so full of love and joy.[141]

For those who have repented of their abortions, Christ offers total forgiveness and healing in the Sacrament of Confession.

Martyrs

During his *EWTN Live* television program focusing on the apparitions of Our Lady of Kibeho on November 24, 2021, Fr. Mitch Pacwa, SJ said that 304 million people died in the twentieth century from wars and genocides. Many of these casualties were Christians at the mercy of Hitler, Stalin, Mao, and Pol Pot. Of these 304 million deaths, how many were classified as martyrs? Reporter Edward Pentin writes that *Salviamo I Cristiani*, or Save the Christians, is an association of Italian Catholic and pro-life groups that studied this issue and concluded:

No other group (Christians) is more persecuted: Out of every 100 people who suffer violations to their right to religious freedom, 75 are Christians. It added that during the course of history, an estimated 70 million Christians have been martyred for their faith, including 40 million in the 20th century alone. Each year, it is said there are 105,000 new Christian martyrs killed by Islamic terrorists, Hindu extremists in India, or Communists in China, North Korea and Vietnam.[142]

Christian martyrdom continues in many nations. Future martyrdom, especially the death of Catholics in America, is known only to God alone. In recent years, church property and statues have been desecrated. At the same time, aggressive actions by civil leaders have limited church attendance or kept them closed altogether as seen at the start of the COVID-19 pandemic. Sadly, our churches were deemed "non-essential" while liquor stores, abortion clinics, and big box stores were deemed "essential," resulting in no restrictions.

The Cloister and a Word on Prophecy

Our Lady also warned that the nuns in the Quito cloister will be few in number and will endure severe difficulties, such as being evicted by the government. This threat has loomed through the years, including recently. But Mother Mariana was up for the challenge. She was chosen by God to serve the sisters and to intercede for the future of the world.

A word on prophecy may be helpful. Prophecy is conditional and things can be altered if people respond to God's will in time. The Scripture enlightens us on this truth. The prophetic word Jonah was called to preach to the enemy of Israel — the Ninevites — resulted in the true repentance of the people. In Fatima, revelation shows that the Second World War could have been avoided or lessened if true conversion occurred. Unfortunately, many people wait until a major catastrophic event or even a brush with their own mortality before they return to God.

Darkness before the Dawn

Chastisements, plagues, famines, domestic conflicts, international disputes, apostasy, a formidable war, and the apparent triumph of evil are all named in the prophecy. Many of these descriptors are common news headlines for our trouble-laden world. Yet when all hope seems lost, we are told of Our Lady's intervention in God's plan for restoration.

Through Adam and Eve, sin entered the world, and through the second Eve, our Blessed Mother working with her Divine Son, the second Adam, the evil one is conquered and chained. With God's grace, we can rid ourselves of Satan's tyranny, which is behind all the deception, conflict, and bloodshed in our world. And even though Christ has defeated sin and death, many still refuse to believe in Him. Scripture shows us the human condition apart from grace: Jesus answered them, "Truly, truly I say to you, everyone who commits sin is a slave of sin" (John 8:34).

In the Fatima prophecies, the triumph of Our Lady's Immaculate Heart plays a key role in history. On August 6, 1945, the American B-29 bomber *Enola Gay* dropped an atomic bomb on Hiroshima. Even though Japan's defeat was inevitable at that point, intelligence suggested that Japan was not ready to surrender. A writer for the National WWII Museum reports: "American intelligence intercepts revealed that by August 2, Japan had already deployed more than 560,000 soldiers and thousands of suicide planes and boats on the island of Kyushu to meet the expected American invasion of Japan."[143] So the United States dropped the atomic bomb, the first time ever a nuclear weapon had been employed. Less than a mile from the devastating epicenter of the blast, a miracle occurred. A group of people survived both the bomb and the fallout from the atomic explosion. The whole area around them

was completely decimated. No harm was done to the church building or the people inside, as Fr. Apostoli explains:

> When asked how he could account for the incredible situ-
> ation, one of the priests who survived said: "I can only tell
> you that we have always tried to fulfill the message of Our
> Lady of Fatima!" Our Lady provides special protection to
> those who respond fully to her requests.[144]

The triumph is coming! Challenges, trials, and even persecution may
also increase before the dawn arrives. But the important thing is to
avail ourselves of the sacraments, personal prayer, and doing God's
will. More will be discussed on the triumph in the last chapter.

Our Lady earlier alluded to the indifference of the wealthy, which
will be explored here. But first, we should look at the generosity of
wealthy Christians. At Franciscan University, a variety of campus
buildings have served the students for decades. Several of these buildings at my alma mater were primarily funded by one wealthy individual. Another apostolate has been substantially helped to evangelize
many because of a wealthy donor. Many vital Catholic institutions
have been blessed by great donors, though many more are needed.

On a global level, many wealthy individuals could make significant impacts on our deteriorating cultures but do not because of
neglect and indifference. They witness the oppression, the persecution of virtue, and evil being financed by enemies of the Church, but
they refuse to respond. Unfortunately, this does apply to people of all
income brackets.

It is easy for many of us to become desensitized to evil because
it is all around us. And sometimes, it does not directly affect us.
While we cannot engage on every front, we must recognize that we
are in a great spiritual battle against principalities, powers, and diabolical intelligence (see Eph. 6:10–20). The Didache Bible gives us a
good understanding of the meaning of God's word here:

> Christians must be fully committed to the Gospel and take advantage of every spiritual resource if they are to rise victorious in the battle against evil ... which must be fought with the spiritual weapons given to us by God and include the truth and righteousness of the Gospel; the practice of the Faith; meditation on the Word of God; and prayer, particularly intercessory prayer ... it is the task of the Christian to imbue every aspect of our lives with prayer in addition to prayer at set times.[145]

Prayer is the greatest weapon in the war against evil, and for many, it is the only weapon they use. More than ever, Christ wants us to pray for our brothers and sisters who are being persecuted in over seventy countries, and even martyred. These suffering Christians need our prayers. Besides a life of prayer, Christians have an obligation to spread the gospel as commanded by Christ in His great commission (see Matt. 28:19–29). Fr. Apostoli highlights the necessity of action in the fight against evil:

> One of the things we must be absolutely convinced of is that Our Lady is calling each one of us to be involved in this struggle. Convictions produce doers. Someone once said: "One person with a belief is equal in force to 99 people who merely have an interest."[146]

During World War II, many Americans were involved in the fight for their country and the needs of their communities, especially as goods became scarce. Tires were the first commodity to be rationed in 1941. This was followed by sugar and gasoline in 1942. Meats, butter, cheese, coffee, and canned fish joined the list. For a little money, families would bring in tinfoil, paper, rags, and grease for the war effort. Everyone was called on to help. Messages on signs were posted all over the country. One sign during the war read: "Food is a Weapon—Don't Waste It!" The caption read: "Buy wisely, cook carefully, eat it all."

Another sign read: "Save Scrap for Victory! Save Metals, Save Paper, Save Rubber, Save Rags."

World War II may be long past, but we are in the midst of the greatest war in the history of the world: the spiritual battle. Sacred Scripture and various Marian apparitions, such as Our Lady of Good Success, confirm this reality. The stakes are higher than ever because they involve the salvation of souls. We must use our resources wisely and employ all of our weapons (prayer, the sacraments, fasting, and the spiritual and corporal works of mercy).

In this war, there are many fronts. Some will serve at their local food pantry or in their parish as lectors, ushers, or council members. Others will volunteer at crisis pregnancy centers or other pro-life apostolates. For some, this fight will require defending children against perverse sex education programs in their local schools. Many will find a ministry in providing trustworthy Catholic books to help evangelize and catechize family and friends. And everyone is called to ongoing conversion and holiness as Scripture and the Second Vatican Council exhorts us. Spiritual warfare is all around us; God is inviting each of us to enlist in His army by serving Him in all the ways He desires. Sometimes we may find ourselves in a country that gets involved in a shooting war with another country. Here our primary resource is calling out to Our Lord and Our Lady for peace as the wheels of war begin to churn.

CHAPTER SEVEN

The 1941 Miracle

The Miracle of the Statue of Our Lady of Good Success of the Purification

IT WAS CALLED THE "War of '41." While the entire world was at war, the War of '41 involved only Ecuador and Peru with no connection to the European or Pacific conflicts. Instead, this war involved disputed land on the border. The people were tense. The old wound of division between the countries was being reopened once again. In fact, the situation kept escalating. War was in the air. A writer for *Military History Now* explains:

> Tensions deepened the following decade. By the early 1940s, Peru moved a sizeable portion of its 68,000-man army up to the border with its estranged neighbor in expectation of a military confrontation. For its part, Ecuador began mobilizing as well. Its entire cabinet resigned *en masse* to take up arms in the fight that was surely coming.[147]

The mismatch was apparent. Ecuador had the smaller and weaker forces against the formidable professional Peruvian army. Strangely, even though it was separate from the world war, Peru had soldiers dressed in "French uniforms, supported by Czech tanks, Italian artillery and American fighter planes doing battle against an enemy armed with German rifles and 19th Century European field guns."[148] So, it is very understandable that the Ecuadoreans were worried.

The war began on Saturday, July 5, 1941. Many casualties were reported early on in the war. Dr. Horvat writes:

> The archbishop of Quito, Carlos Maria Javier de la Torre, ordered that a *Triduum* of prayers be said in all the churches of Quito addressing the Blessed Virgin to implore her intercession before God to end the hostilities. On July 24, the *Triduum* in honor of Our Lady of Good Success started in the Church of the Immaculate Conception in downtown Quito.[149]

The faithful of Quito and the surrounding regions gathered to beseech God and their Mother for peace. Bishop Carlos had the statue of Our Lady of Good Success of the Purification brought out. At the 10:30 a.m. Mass, during the elevation of the Host. Matthew Arnold describes a miracle:

> The statue was seen to open and close her eyes; turning her gaze from the sisters in the lower choir — directly adjacent to the sanctuary — then up to heaven. It was as though she was saying, "Your prayers are being taken before the Divine Majesty."[150]

This was witnessed by more than thirty thousand people.[151] News quickly spread throughout the nation. On July 28, 1941, the top newspaper of Quito, *El Comercio,* the daily newspaper *Ultimas Noticias,* and *El Telegrafo* of Guayaquil all carried the headlines and story. Six other newspapers and publications also reported the miraculous account, which happened repeatedly for about sixteen hours.[152]

When this phenomenon happened, it greatly consoled and gave the Ecuadoreans new hope. *El Comercio* reported:

> From ten o'clock in the morning of yesterday, in the most central location of this capital city, the Plaza of Independence, on one of the corners where the old Church of the

Immaculate Conception stands; it is heard from mouth to mouth that the Virgin of Good Success, in whose honor religious services were being carried out for three days with much enthusiasm, had opened her eyes and raised them to heaven on several occasions.[153]

In the Church of the Immaculate Conception, located on that same plaza square where Don Gabriel Garcia Moreno had left the cathedral to return to his office and was assassinated, the miracle took place. Dr. Horvat describes the details this way:

> Various ladies were near the main altar praying to Our Lady when they observed that the Statue of the Virgin of Good Success opened her eyes wide, turned them downward at them with a look of great compassion and, then, raised them upward. This happened several times. Visibly moved by the miraculous event, they remained in prayer, several of them weeping, but they did not tell the others present in the church what they had witnessed.[154]

When the chaplain of the Conceptionist convent, Fr. Benjamin Rafael Ayora y Cueva, arrived to say Mass, he stopped to pray before the statue. He had a devotion to Our Lady of Good Success of the Purification. He witnessed the same miracle. He was deeply moved but thought he was experiencing an optical illusion. He went to tell the ladies who were praying nearby, and they confirmed his experience. They had seen the same miracle about an hour earlier.[155]

News of the miracle spread rapidly, and soon, thousands made their way to the church — not far from where Mother Mariana first experienced the apparitions long ago. *El Telegrafo* published their news piece and related that an "enormous number of faithful and onlookers came" to witness the miracle firsthand and considered it "as a new religious miracle *in these times of transcendental importance for the international life of the country*."[156] The Guayaquil daily newspaper, *El Universo*, reported that by evening "a large crowd" of "2,000" wanted to see the Virgin and tried to force open the door of the church, but the police stopped them from harming the door.[157]

Another newspaper, *La Sociedad*, on August 3, 1941, reported an interesting incident that happened with two university students:

> Among the countless people attending, there were some who did not see it, while the majority did. A curious case is that of the university students, one of whom was thoroughly Catholic, but the other was a Socialist. They came in out of curiosity to observe the phenomenon about which everyone was talking. The Catholic did not see anything, while the Socialist was going from one emotion to another upon seeing the opening and closing of the statue's eyes, until he fell on his knees bathed in tears.[158]

At Fatima, approximately seventy thousand believers, skeptics, unbelievers, and the curious witnessed the great miracle of the sun. Fr. Apostoli summarizes the various human responses to the day the "sun danced:"

> Many who came believing in the apparitions were strengthened in their faith. Some who were skeptical had their doubts removed, many of the curious went away believers. Of those who did not believe, perhaps some simply refused to do so, despite what they witnessed. Perhaps they did not want to see what others saw.[159]

Sometimes a grace needed by one person is not necessary for another person. God's providence directs all things as He sees fit. As at Fatima, many eyewitness testimonies about the miracle at Quito were given, including priests, lawyers, doctors, students, notable men and women, religious sisters, pious people, indifferent people, and even skeptics.[160]

A reporter for *El Comercio* interviewed witnesses for his paper. "He spoke with the distinguished Señora Matilde Chiriboga de Salvador, who told him with great excitement: 'I saw the Blessed Virgin open and close her eyes, just as thousands of persons have seen it today.'"[161] But the reason why the miracle of '41 was unforgettable was due to what happened next.

The prayers of the Ecuadorian people were answered. A ceasefire was called shortly after the Triduum of prayers was completed. Peace returned to their country. Hostilities ceased, and the formal treaty known as the *Rio De Janeiro Protocol* was later signed. But when will the complete restoration of peace promised by Our Lady be realized?

CHAPTER EIGHT

The Restoration

The Really Good News

PROFOUND PEACE AND JOY often occur after someone receives a good report. Perhaps the great news that a conflict has ended as with the War of '41. Or perhaps passing an important exam in order to enter a new career. Or it may be the simple delight of seeing relatives and friends in a homecoming after a long absence.

Sacred Scripture provides the greatest report of hope and peace. Long before Christ preached the good news, Genesis 3:15 prophesized His coming, the first Biblical passage to do such. This passage follows after the human race had fallen into Original Sin through the cunning work of the deceiver. In fact, the passage is called the First Gospel, or *Protoevangelium*. We read in the Scripture this great promise of the coming Messiah, which God addresses to the serpent: "I will put enmity between you and the woman, and between your offspring and hers; he will strike your head, and you will strike his heel" (Gen. 3:15). God had a plan after the Fall to redeem us all. The Didache Bible comments on the verse:

> God promised that the offspring of the woman would defeat Satan. Christians see this promise fulfilled in Mary and her Son, Jesus Christ, whose Death on the Cross and Resurrection conquered sin and death. For this reason, Christ and his Mother are referred to as the New Adam and the New Eve.[162]

The Church Fathers understood Mary's key role in salvation history. Specifically, "Mary is understood as the 'New Eve,' bearing the Redeemer of the world via her 'fiat/yes' (Luke 1:37), whereas the first Eve failed to trust and obey God," according to apologist and writer Tom Nash's observations on the Fathers.[163] Jesus inflicted the mortal wound on Satan (crushed or bruised the serpent's head), who had been behind so much of humanity's woes (struck or bruised his heel). Apologist Jimmy Akin further explains Genesis 3:15:

> She, not anyone else, was the person who agreed to become the human channel through which Christ would enter the world in order to crush the serpent's head (Lk 1:38). She herself was wounded when the serpent struck Jesus. Simeon had prophesied to her that 'a sword will pierce through your own soul also,' a prophecy fulfilled when Mary saw her Son hanging from the cross (Jn 19:25–27).[164]

Those who accept Christ and His teachings are those spoken about in 1 John 5:5: "Who is it that conquers the world but the one who believes that Jesus is the Son of God?" Catholics defeat the evil one and his minions through faith in the Son of God, who alone is victorious.

In the story of Our Lady of Good Success and Our Lady of Fatima, the triumph of the two Hearts (the Sacred Heart of Jesus and the Immaculate Heart of Mary) is rooted in Genesis 3:15. St. Paul wrote of this Good News: "For I am not ashamed of the gospel; it is the power of God for salvation to everyone who has faith" (Rom. 1:16). This restoration of the Catholic Church is possible because of Christ's redemption. No scandal or crisis can destroy her.

The tables were turned on Satan! And out of the great suffering of the Passion, Death, and Resurrection of the Lord — in the redemption — victory has been achieved for all. Christ formed the Church to continue His saving mission in the world.

The great future restoration brings tranquility to the Church and the nations after the chaos. The crisis itself was caused by the spread of sin throughout the world and the resulting darkness, divisions, and disorders. The promise of peace is a hallmark of Our Lady's major prophetic messages and a call for our response. The restoration is the time when Our Lady steps in and vanquishes the devil and his minions in our world. Peace is restored in this period and the faithful remain to rebuild Christian civilization.

The Promised Peace

Mary said that In order to dissipate this black cloud that prevents the Church from enjoying the clear day of liberty, there will be a formidable and frightful war, which will see the bloodshed of countrymen and foreigners, of secular and regular priests and of religious. That night will be most horrible, she said, for, humanly speaking, evil will seem to triumph.

This, then, Mary said, will mark the arrival of her hour, when she, in a marvelous way, will dethrone the proud and cursed Satan, trampling him under her feet and fettering him in the infernal abyss. Thus, she promised, the Church and Country will finally be free of his cruel tyranny.[165]

The promised period of peace via Our Lady's intervention comes after a terrible war. The peace is also implied in the dethroning of Satan and the end of his reign of tyranny. It is interesting to note that the prophecy on the great war and the dethroning of the devil specifically references the trampling of Satan under Mary's feet. At Fatima, Our Lady promised that her Immaculate Heart would triumph, and a period of peace would be granted to the world with the Holy Father's consecration of Russia and the practice of the Five First Saturday Communions of Reparation. Pope St. John Paul II made the consecration in 1984, and it was accepted by Heaven according to Sr. Lucia, who was the only living Fatima seer at the time. Sr. Lucia stated in 1991 that we need to continue the First Saturdays, the Rosary, and penance as we await the promised triumph. Tumults, trials, and Church scandals can still become worse before peace reigns.

Strength and Virtue

In the current period of apostasy, there are many pressures to conform, compromise moral truths, and embrace the opinions of faithless men in order to gain favor or avoid confrontations. Overcoming fear in the face of these strong pressures is paramount for the sake of souls. In the apparition of 1634 below, Our Lady — as a loving Mother — mentions the strengths and virtues that we should cultivate, especially in our troubled times. Dr. Horvat translates a part of the Virgin's message that underscores how to help those wrapped up in false doctrines:

> In order to free men from bondage to these heresies, those whom the merciful love of my Most Holy Son will designate for that restoration will need great strength of will, constancy, valor and confidence in God. To test this faith and confidence of the just, there will be occasions when all will seem to be lost and paralyzed. This will be, then, the happy beginning of the complete restoration.[166]

These virtues listed by Our Lady are even more crucial in these intense times when Christ longs for the restoration of His Church and above all, each person. Someone has well stated that *courage is fear that has said its prayers*!

How Are We to Live Now?

Msgr. Charles Pope wrote that we should not book a ticket on a sinking ship, which is what we do when we make this world our priority. He reminds us of what is truly lasting: "Too many people root their lives in passing things. The challenge for us is to root our lives in the word and Kingdom of God, which remains forever."[167] Doing our daily duties while keeping an eternal perspective builds the kingdom.

Over four hundred years have passed since Our Lady of Good Success appeared to an obscure nun in Ecuador. As the world has sunk into greater darkness and these prophecies became fulfilled in our times, Our Lady gave several other important messages in the twentieth century. Specifically, Our Lady told us at Fatima, Portugal (1917), at Akita, Japan (1971), and at Kibeho, Rwanda (1981) to pray the Rosary daily. In Kibeho, she asked for the Rosary of the Seven Sorrows or the traditional Rosary to be prayed. The Rosary is a most excellent meditation on the Gospels and a powerful weapon to bring sinners back to God. Also attending Mass and receiving the Eucharist as often as possible combined with the Rosary are proven ways to heed these prophecies and grow in strength and charity.

In addition to praying the daily Rosary, Our Lady calls us to make sacrifices for the conversion of sinners, especially offering up our sufferings. Prayer, penance, offering up suffering, and leading good lives were at the heart of Fatima's message.[168] In the Gospels, Our Lord exhorts us to perform various spiritual and corporal works of mercy depending on our state in life. Both works of mercy are fruitful!

God's Punctuation Marks!

Over the course of time, God will often put a punctuation mark on a saintly person's life. This is my term for God's way of giving us a sign regarding a person. In Quito, in 1906, during some remodeling work at the convent, Mother Mariana's and the other founding mother's coffins were opened and these sisters were found to be incorrupt. Remember, Mother Mariana passed away on January 16, 1635 — 271 years before! Based on the laws of science, her body should have decomposed, becoming mere bones and ashes. Some saintly bodies, however, do not return to dust. In Mother Mariana's case, a heavenly sign appears to have been given.

In 1986, Msgr. Luis E. Cadena y Almeida was selected as the postulator to pursue the cause of beatification of the Servant of God, Mother Mariana Francisca of Jesus Torres y Berriochoa. The life of this remarkable and holy Conceptionist sister continues to inspire our times as do the prophetic messages given by Our Lady of Good Success to her. Although Our Lady of Good Success of the Purification spoke many dire messages for our times, prophecy is not set in stone. Catholics and other Christians today can change the course of future generations if we become intercessors like Mother Mariana and respond wholeheartedly to God's will. Chastisements can be mitigated by our response. The daily rosary, frequent reception of the sacraments, and leading good lives will help us navigate even the most dreadful of storms!

Endnotes

1 Manuel Sousa Pereira, *The Story of Our Lady of Good Success and Novena*, Abridged Edition, trans. Rev. Paul Kimball (Camillus, New York: Dolorosa Press, 2013), iii.

2 Luis E. Cadena y Almeida, *A Spanish Mystic in Quito: Sor Mariana de Jesus Torres* (Hanover, PA: The Foundation for a Christian Civilization, Inc., 1990), 5.

3 Pereira, *The Story of Our Lady of Good Success and Novena*, iii.

4 Mrs. Maxwell-Scott, *Gabriel Garcia Moreno* (New York, NY: Benziger Brothers, 1910), 1–2.

5 Marian Therese Horvat, *Our Lady of Good Success*, Fifth Edition (Los Angeles, CA: Tradition in Action, Inc., 2015), 25.

6 Ibid.

7 Cadena y Almeida, *A Spanish Mystic in Quito*, 1.

8 Horvat, *Our Lady of Good Success*, 24.

9 Cadena y Almeida, *A Spanish Mystic in Quito*, 2.

10 Ibid., 2–3.

11 Pereira, *The Story of Our Lady of Good Success and Novena*, iv.

12 Peter V. N. Henderson, *Gabriel Garcia Moreno and Conservative State Formation in the Andes* (Austin, TX: University of Texas Press, 2008), 7.

13 Maxwell-Scott, *Gabriel Garcia Moreno*, 48–49.

14 Cadena y Almeida, *A Spanish Mystic in Quito*, 12.

15 Ibid.

16 Pereira, *The Story of Our Lady of Good Success and Novena*, iii.

17 Cadena y Almeida, *A Spanish Mystic in Quito*, 17.

18 Ibid., 18.

19 Ibid.

20 Pereira, *The Story of Our Lady of Good Success and Novena*, 1.

21 Ibid., 60–61 (paraphrase).

22 Ibid., 1. Fr. Pereira refers to Sister Mariana as Mother Mariana, though at the time of this revelation, she had not been elected Mother Superior.

23 Horvat, *Our Lady of Good Success*, 26.

24 Cadena y Almeida, *A Spanish Mystic in Quito*, 24–28.

25 Pereira, *The Story of Our Lady of Good Success and Novena*, 1 (paraphrase).

26 Horvat, *Our Lady of Good Success*, 27.

27 Pereira, *The Story of Our Lady of Good Success and Novena*, 2.

28 Ibid.

29 Horvat, *Our Lady of Good Success*, 28.

30 Russell Shaw, ed., *Our Sunday Visitor's Encyclopedia of Catholic Doctrine* (Huntington, IN: Our Sunday Visitor Publishing Division, 1997), 278.

31 John Walters, "Communism Killed 94M in the 20th Century, Feels Need to Kill Again," *reason*, March 13, 2013, https://reason.com/2013/03/13/communism-killed-94m-in-20th-century/.

32 Paul Kengor, *A Pope and a President* (Wilmington, DE: ISI Books, Intercollegiate Studies Institute, 2017), 56.

33 Ibid., 59.

34 Ibid.

35 Andrew Apostoli, *Fatima for Today* (San Francisco, CA: Ignatius Press, 2010), 219.

36 Ibid.

37 "China," United States Commission on International Religious Freedom, accessed September 7, 2023, https://www.uscirf.gov/countries/china.

38 Steve Weatherbe, "Oklahoma Satanist gives up plan to desecrate Eucharist: Archbishop withdraws lawsuit," *Lifesite News*, August 22, 2014, www.lifesitenews.com.

39 Apostoli, *Fatima for Today*, 219–220.

40 "How has porn impacted our Society and our Culture," Road to Purity, www.roadtopurity.com/how-porn-destroys-society.

41 "How Porn is Destroying our Society and Your Family," Road to Purity, www.roadtopurity.com/how-porn-destroys-society.

42 Luke Gilkerson, "How Many Women are Hooked on Porn? 10 Stats that May Shock You," Covenant Eyes, September 3, 2015, www.covenanteyes.com.

43 "So What's Wrong with Porn," Road to Purity, www.roadtopurity.com/how-porn-destroys-society.

44 "How has porn impacted our Society and our Culture," Road to Purity, www.roadtopurity.com/how-porn-destroys-society.

45 "Clear Your Eyes & Mind of Porn | Steve Pokorny on The Dr J Show ep. 92," Ruth Institute, July 23, 2021, video, 54:30, https://www.youtube.com/watch?v=L-92QNdE4qk.

46 Pereira, *The Story of Our Lady of Good Success and Novena*, 8.

47 Ibid., 7.

48 Horvat, *Our Lady of Good Success*, 31.

49 Cadena y Almeida, *A Spanish Mystic in Quito*, 31.

50 Horvat, *Our Lady of Good Success*, 31.

51 Cadena y Almeida, *A Spanish Mystic in Quito*, 33 (paraphrase).

52 Ibid.

53 Ibid.

54 Ibid., 34 (paraphrase).

55 Matthew Arnold, *Mary of Good Success and the Restoration of the Church* (Matthew Arnold, 2019), 23.

56 Cadena y Almeida, *A Spanish Mystic in Quito*, 34.

57 Ibid., 39.

58 Horvat, *Our Lady of Good Success*, 32.

59 Ibid., 33.

60 Kathleen Beckman, *A Family Guide to Spiritual Warfare* (Manchester, NH: Sophia Institute Press, 2020), 13.

61 Russell Shaw, ed., *Our Sunday Visitor's Encyclopedia of Catholic Doctrine*, 710.

62 Pereira, *The Story of Our Lady of Good Success and Novena*, 17.

63 Ibid., 18 (paraphrase).

64 Ibid., 18–21 (paraphrase).

65 Arnold, *Mary of Good Success and the Restoration of the Church*, 11.

66 Pereira, *The Story of Our Lady of Good Success and Novena*, 49 (paraphrase).

67 Arnold, *Mary of Good Success and the Restoration of the Church*, 13.

68 Horvat, *Our Lady of Good Success*, 50.

69 Ibid.

70 Cadena y Almeida, *A Spanish Mystic in Quito*, 63.

71 Maxwell-Scott, *Gabriel Garcia Moreno*, 6.

72 Ibid., 15 (paraphrase).

73 Ibid., 135–136.

74 Augustine Berthe, *Garcia Moreno*, trans. Paul M. Kimball (Dolorosa Press, 2006), 60.

75 Ibid., 61.

76 Ibid., 62–63.

77 Ibid., 62.

78 Ibid., 74.

79 Maxwell-Scott, *Gabriel Garcia Moreno*, 9–10.

80 Berthe, *Garcia Moreno*, 77.

81 Joseph F. X. Sladky, "A Statesman After God's Own Heart: Gabriel Garcia Moreno," *Crisis Magazine*, August 9, 2012.

82 Berthe, *Garcia Moreno*, 151.

83 Ibid., 152 (paraphrase).

84 Ibid.

85 Michael Chad Shibler, "Gabriel Garcia Moreno--Faith, Order and Progress," *Crusade*, July/August, 2010, 11.

86 Berthe, *Garcia Moreno*, 157.

87 Sladky, "A Stateman After God's Own Heart."

88 Ibid.

89 Shibler, "Gabriel Garcia Moreno--Faith, Order and Progress," 11.

90 Berthe, *Garcia Moreno*, 157.

91   Frank M. Rega, "The Greatest Catholic President: Garcia Moreno of Ecuador," *Christian Order* 5, 6, 7 (2008), http://members.aol.com/fmrega7/GarciaMoreno.htm.

92   Berthe, *Garcia Moreno*, 158.

93   Ibid., 110.

94   Sladky, "A Stateman After God's Own Heart."

95   Berthe, *Garcia Moreno*, 259 (paraphrase).

96   Shibler, "Gabriel Garcia Moreno--Faith, Order and Progress," 11.

97   Sladky, "A Stateman After God's Own Heart."

98   Berthe, *Garcia Moreno*, 260 (paraphrase).

99   Ibid.

100 Maxwell-Scott, *Gabriel Garcia Moreno*, 14.

101 Wikipedia, s.v. "Gabriel Garcia Moreno," last modified August 22, 2023, wikipedia.org/wiki/Gabriel_Garcia_Moreno.

102 Sladky, "A Stateman After God's Own Heart."

103 Gary Potter, "Gabriel Garcia Moreno, Statesman and Martyr," Catholicism.org, August 1, 2007, https://Catholicism.org.

104 Sladky, "A Stateman After God's Own Heart" (paraphrase).

105 Ibid.

106 Berthe, *Garcia Moreno*, 163.

107 Ibid., 164 (paraphrase).

108 Ibid., 302.

109 Sladky, "A Stateman After God's Own Heart."

110 Shibler, "Gabriel Garcia Moreno--Faith, Order and Progress," 11.

111 "Biography of Gabriel Garcia Moreno," Our Lady of Good Success website, accessed September 7, 2023, https://www.ourladyofgoodsuccess.com/pages/biography-of-gabriel-garcia-moreno?_pos=1&_sid=ab1a6ccfe&_ss=r.

112 Berthe, *Garcia Moreno*, 316.

113 Maxwell-Scott, *Gabriel Garcia Moreno*, 152–153.

114 Berthe, *Garcia Moreno*, 319–320.

115 Laura Wood, "The Sacred Heart and Political Order," The Thinking Housewife (blog), June 27, 2014, https://www.thinkinghousewife.com/2014/06/the-sacred-heart-and-political-order/.

116 Ibid.

117 Shibler, "Gabriel Garcia Moreno--Faith, Order and Progress," 12.

118 Marian T. Horvat, "The Last Day of Gabriel Garcia Moreno," Tradition in Action, February 25, 2011, https://www.traditioninaction.org/OLGS/A011olgsQuito_Garcia_1.htm.

119 Berthe, *Garcia Moreno*, 322–323.

120 Ibid., 323 (paraphrase).

121 Horvat, "The Last Day of Gabriel Garcia Moreno."

122 Sladky, "A Stateman After God's Own Heart."

123 Miracle Hunter Website, http://miraclehunter.com/.

124 Manuel Sousa Pereira, *The Admirable Life of Mother Mariana*, vol. II, trans. Marian T. Horvat (Los Angeles, CA: Tradition in Action, 2006), 16–21 (paraphrase).

125 Ibid., 21–22.

126 Ralph Martin, *The Urgency of the New Evangelization: Answering the Call* (Huntington, IN: Our Sunday Visitor Publishing Division, 2013), 16.

127 Pereira, *The Admirable Life of Mother Mariana*, 22.

128 Ibid., 22–23.

129 Bob Ellis, "Saving the Family during Revolutionary Times," Fatima Blog, August 14, 2020, www.bluearmy.com.

130 Pope John Paul II, Apostolic Exhortation *Familiaris Consortio* (November 22, 1981), no. 75.

131 Arnold, *Mary of Good Success and the Restoration of the Church*, 29.

132 Ibid., 29–30.

133 Pereira, *The Admirable Life of Mother Mariana*, 23.

134 Ralph Martin, *A Church in Crisis-Pathways Forward* (Steubenville, OH: Emmaus Road Publishing, 2020), 298–299.

135 Arnold, *Mary of Good Success and the Restoration of the Church*, 28–29.

136 Cadena y Almeida, *A Spanish Mystic in Quito*, 97–100.

137 "Infanticide in the Ancient World," Early Church History (blog), https://earlychurchhistory.org/medicine/infanticide-in-the-ancient-world/.

138 Austin Ruse, *Under Siege--No Finer Time to Be a Faithful Catholic* (Manchester, NH: Crisis Publications, 2021), 87.

139 Annamarie Adkins, "Priestly Identity: Crisis and Renewal," A Zenit Daily Dispatch, March 19, 2008, www.ewtn.com.

140 Ruse, *Under Siege--No Finer Time to Be a Faithful Catholic*, 98 (exact quote and paraphrase).

141 "Quotes from Mother Teresa on Abortion," www.stjoanofarcchurch.org.

142 Edward Pentin, "Rally Spotlights Persecution Against Christians," A Zenit Daily Dispatch, July 19, 2012, www.ewtn.com.

143 "The Most Fearsome Sight: The Atomic Bombing of Hiroshima," August 6, 2020, www.nationalww2museum.org.

144 Apostoli, *Fatima for Today*, 227.

145 *The Didache Bible* (San Francisco: Ignatius Press, 2015).

146 Apostoli, *Fatima for Today*, 228–229.

147 "Ecuadorian-Peruvian War of 1941--Inside the Strange South American Conflict that Raged While Europe Burned," Military History Now, September 26, 2012, https://militaryhistorynow.com/2019/06/27/sideshow-peru-fights-ecuador-during-ww2s-darkest-summer/.

148 Ibid.

149 Marian Therese Horvat, "Our Lady of Good Success Raises and Lowers Her Eyes," Tradition in Action, www.traditioninaction.org.

150 Arnold, *Mary of Good Success and the Restoration of the Church*, 21–22.

151 Manuel Sousa Pereira, *The Story of Our Lady of Good Success and Novena*, trans. Paul Kimball (Camillus, NY: Dolorosa Press, 2013), 156.

152 Ibid., 157–173 (paraphrase).

153 Ibid., 157.

154 Horvat, "Our Lady of Good Success Raises and Lowers Her Eyes."

155 Ibid. (paraphrase).

156 Pereira, *The Story of Our Lady of Good Success and Novena*, 160.

157 Ibid., 160–161.

158 Ibid., 166.

159 Apostoli, *Fatima for Today*, 129.

160 Pereira, *The Story of Our Lady of Good Success and Novena*, 166 (paraphrase).

161 Horvat, "Our Lady of Good Success Raises and Lowers Her Eyes."

162 The Didache Bible, 7.

163 Tom Nash, "Genesis 3:15: Who Crushes the Serpent's Head?," Catholic Answers, www.catholic.com.

164 Jimmy Akin, "Who Will Crush the Serpent's Head?," Catholic Answers, September 1, 1997, www.catholic.com.

165 Horvat, *Our Lady of Good Success*, 59.

166 Ibid., 55.

167 Charles Pope, "The World Will Pass Away, But Jesus Christ Wins," *National Catholic Register*, November 7, 2021, 16.

168 Apostoli, *Fatima for Today*, 230–231 (paraphrase).

About the Author

JAMES VALOIS, THE FATHER of two adult children, reverted to the Catholic Faith from Evangelicalism while a student at Franciscan University, where he earned a B.A. in theology. He has worked in business, in youth ministry, and in teaching and administrative roles. His articles and book reviews have appeared in the *Wanderer*, *Soul Magazine*, and *Catholic Life Magazine*.

Sophia Institute

SOPHIA INSTITUTE IS A nonprofit institution that seeks to nurture the spiritual, moral, and cultural life of souls and to spread the gospel of Christ in conformity with the authentic teachings of the Roman Catholic Church.

Sophia Institute Press fulfills this mission by offering translations, reprints, and new publications that afford readers a rich source of the enduring wisdom of mankind.

Sophia Institute also operates the popular online resource CatholicExchange.com. *Catholic Exchange* provides world news from a Catholic perspective as well as daily devotionals and articles that will help readers to grow in holiness and live a life consistent with the teachings of the Church.

In 2013, Sophia Institute launched Sophia Institute for Teachers to renew and rebuild Catholic culture through service to Catholic education. With the goal of nurturing the spiritual, moral, and cultural life of souls, and an abiding respect for the role and work of teachers, we strive to provide materials and programs that are at once enlightening to the mind and ennobling to the heart; faithful and complete, as well as useful and practical.

Sophia Institute gratefully recognizes the Solidarity Association for preserving and encouraging the growth of our apostolate over the course of many years. Without their generous and timely support, this book would not be in your hands.

www.SophiaInstitute.com
www.CatholicExchange.com
www.SophiaInstituteforTeachers.org

Sophia Institute Press is a registered trademark of Sophia Institute.
Sophia Institute is a tax-exempt institution as defined by the
Internal Revenue Code, Section 501(c)(3). Tax ID 22-2548708.